NATIONAL GEOGRAPHIC
KiDS

weird
but
true!

2018

Published by Collins
An imprint of HarperCollins Publishers
Westerhill Road
Bishopbriggs
Glasgow G64 2QT
www.harpercollins.co.uk

In association with National Geographic Partners, LLC

NATIONAL GEOGRAPHIC and the Yellow Border Design are trademarks of
the National Geographic Society and used under license.

National Geographic Kids Weird But True & Design are trademarks of
National Geographic Society and used under license.

First published 2017

ISBN 978-0-00-796499-4

10 9 8 7 6 5 4 3 2 1

A catalogue record for this book is available from the British Library

Printed in Great Britain by Bell & Bain Ltd, Glasgow

If you would like to comment on any aspect of this book, please contact
us at the above address or online.
natgeokidsbooks.co.uk
collins.reference@harpercollins.co.uk

NATIONAL GEOGRAPHIC KiDS

weird but true! 2018

wild & wacky facts & photos!

contents

Most hailstones measure about 5 mm (0.2 in). Not all are that small though – go to page 10 to find out about some *slightly* bigger ones.

Hailstones can grow to the size of **golf balls**.

CHAPTER 1

AMaZiNg EaRTh

Do you dare?

Are you BRAVE ENOUGH to visit the WORLD'S LARGEST CAVE, Hang Sơn Đoòng, in VIETNAM?

You could easily slot St Paul's Cathedral – with Westminster Abbey on top – into its entrance chamber, which is more than 200 m (660 ft) high and 150 m (490 ft) wide. The cave narrows and twists into passages that run for 9 km (5.6 mi). Incredibly, it was almost unknown until 2009, when a team of brave British cavers explored its extraordinary inner depths.

Your visit starts with an 80 m (260 ft) scramble down some rocks to the floor of an underground forest. As you explore you might see monkeys, flying foxes, bats, and pools of luminous algae. The cave also has unknown plant species, rare cave pearls, the tallest stalagmite in the world measuring 70 m (230 ft), and its own crashing river complete with waterfalls. Just remember to take a big packed lunch...

BATMAN

WOULD LOVE THIS PLACE

Beware the
WEATHER

Hail is formed in tall thunderclouds. Hail is usually only 5 mm (0.2 in) across, but in extreme cases it can grow to 15 cm (6 in) and weigh more than 0.5 kg (1.1 lb). >>>

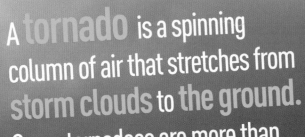

A tornado is a spinning column of air that stretches from storm clouds to the ground. Some tornadoes are more than 3 km (2 mi) wide and can spin up to 480 km/h (300 mph). They usually only last 10 minutes but can be very destructive.

<<<

Hurricanes are known as **Cyclones** in the **South Pacific** and as **Typhoons** in the **North west Pacific.**

∧
∧ **Hurricanes** can reach 2,000 km (1,200 mi) in diameter. They rotate
∧ anticlockwise in the northern hemisphere and clockwise in the southern hemisphere. Hurricanes have strong winds, heavy rain, and a storm surge.

∨
∨ **Flash flooding** is caused when a lot of rain falls in a very short time.
∨

11

WHO LEFT THE LIGHTS ON?

An **AURORA** is a spectacular natural light show.

The sun constantly emits high-energy particles into space. This invisible stream of electrons and protons is called the solar wind. The solar wind squeezes Earth's magnetic field, which builds up energy. Sometimes this is released, and a flurry of electrons zoom around the planet's poles. The electrons hit gas atoms, causing them to emit light. This creates a spectacular aurora. You can usually only see auroras in the Arctic and Antarctic, but sometimes they are visible further south. This image was taken at Loch Lomond, Scotland.

SEISMIC SEA WAVES

In 2011 a **HUGE EARTHQUAKE** near **JAPAN** caused a massive **TSUNAMI** with waves up to **40.5 m (133 ft) HIGH.**

rogue one

In 1995 a laser sensor on the Draupner oil platform recorded a rogue wave that was 25.6 m (84 ft) high – imagine six double-decker buses stacked on top of each other. It was twice as tall as any other wave in the storm.

MEGA WAVES

Playing in the waves at the beach is great fun. BUT WAVES CAN BE A FEARSOME FORCE OF NATURE. Storms, earthquakes, and other disasters can drive waters wild, creating mega waves. Let's take a look at some of the biggest ever.

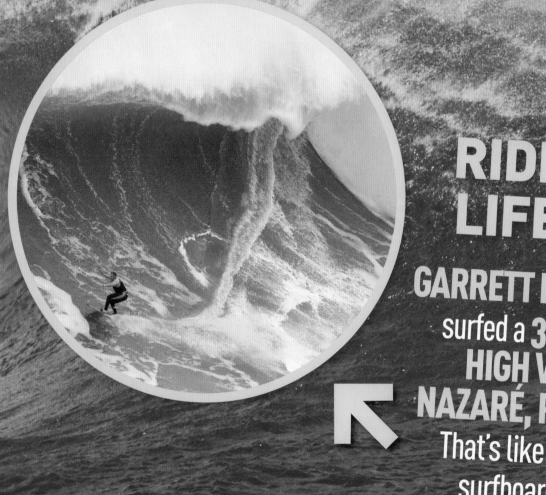

RIDE OF A LIFETIME

GARRETT MCNAMARA surfed a **30 m (100 ft) HIGH WAVE** at **NAZARÉ, PORTUGAL.** That's like riding your surfboard down a **TEN-STOREY BUILDING.**

Ready to **BLOW**

Volatile volcanoes and lightning fast lava

You can normally outrun lava. But the molten rock that flows from Nyiragongo in the Democratic Republic of Congo can speed along at 100 km/h (60 mph). This is because it has very low levels of silica, the mineral that makes most lava so slow and oozy.

In A.D. 79, **Mount Vesuvius** in Italy erupted and buried the cities of Pompeii and Herculaneum under 4-6 m (13-20 ft) of burning ash and pumice killing thousands.

>>>

While most people would run a mile from an erupting volcano, George Kourounis dived deep into the Marum Crater on Vanuatu. Acid rain splashed his protective suit.

HOLIDAY WRECKER

Eyjafjallajökull (that's a mouthful) erupted in 2010. Volcanic ash is bad for planes and especially jet engines. Hundreds of planes were grounded for days over Europe.

You get my drift?

TECTONIC PLATES

Ever noticed how South America and Africa look as if they could fit neatly together? Well, they once did. In 1912, a scientist called Alfred Wegener realised that the continents 'drift' around the world. Planet Earth has layers like an onion. The stiff outer crust is called the lithosphere. It's not a complete shell, but is made up of seven big and many smaller 'tectonic plates'. The continents sit on these plates. Between the crust and the hot inner core is the mantle. As very hot material near the Earth's core rises, cooler mantle rock sinks – imagine a pot of water boiling on a stove. Over very long periods of time, the currents in the swirling mantle make the plates move, and this causes continents to form and break up.

TECTONIC PLATES that carry America and Europe are moving apart at the rate of 3.6 cm (1.42 in) per year, which is roughly the same rate that fingernails grow.

NORTH AMERICAN PLATE

North America

JUAN DE FUCA PLATE

CARIBBEAN PLATE

PACIFIC PLATE

South America

NAZCA PLATE

SOUTH AMERICAN PLATE

SCOTIA PLATE

Nowadays you'd go to the Caribbean, but 350 million years ago, Britain would have been your top tropical destination. It then lay close to the equator in a warm, shallow sea. 150 million years before that, Britain was near the South Pole! Over millions of years, Britain has been a desert, a swamp, a tropical rainforest, and a frozen land trapped under a kilometre of ice.

EURASIAN PLATE

Europe

Asia

PHILIPPINE
SEA
PLATE

PACIFIC
PLATE

ARABIAN
PLATE

INDIAN
PLATE

Africa

AFRICAN PLATE

Oceania

AUSTRALIAN PLATE

ANTARCTIC PLATE

When the
**INDIAN
SUBCONTINENT**
crashed into the Asian continent
40–50 million years ago,
the colliding land was thrust
upwards, creating the Himalayas.
This is still happening so the
mountain peaks are still
growing.

PRINTING THE REEF

Imagine you're in a spaceship orbiting Earth and you look down to see a graceful pale arc 2,300 km (1,400 mi) long in the sea by Australia. That's a huge structure, nearly twice as long as Britain – what can it be?! What advanced civilisation built it? What huge tools did they use? Actually, this wonder of the natural world – the Great Barrier Reef – was constructed by tiny organisms called coral polyps. It took billions upon billions of these little animals 20,000 years to build their megacity. The reef is also home to 30 species of whales, dolphins, and porpoises, as well as sea snakes, turtles, and at least 1,500 species of fish.

But reefs are very fragile ecosystems, easily damaged by pollution and climate change. So scientists at Sydney University are using 3D-printing technology to create prosthetic coral to repair the reef. First, they make a virtual 3D map. This is then used as a template to print a real 3D model reef section. The printed reef has all the nooks, crannies, passages, and doors that fish and sea creatures love. Divers place it on the seabed where baby coral polyps can find it and do what they do best – keep on building.

REEF ↑

3D PRINTER ←

Genghis Khan left behind the largest empire in history when he died. He had a slightly odd request for his burial – flick to page 38 to find out more.

Genghis Kahn didn't allow **paintings, sculptures** or **engravings** of his appearance to be created. The **first depictions** of him were made **after his death.**

CHAPTER 2

TiMe tRaVELLiNG

FOREVER HOMES

CATACOMBS, PARIS, FRANCE

Hidden below the centre of Paris – the catacombs are made up of miles of tunnels containing over six million people's skulls and bones. It's known as the 'Empire of the Dead' because so many people are buried there. You can visit the tunnels for yourself... if you dare!

CITY OF THE DEAD, NORTH OSSETIA, RUSSIA

From a distance it looks like a normal town, but the inhabitants have all been dead for a very, very long time. Inside all the houses are the remains of the town's residents, with all their clothes and belongings. It's thought the people died in a plague over 200 years ago.

THE TAJ MAHAL, AGRA, INDIA

Did you know this beautiful palace was never built for anyone alive to live in? After Mumtaz Mahal died in 1631, her husband Emperor Shah Jahan built the Taj Mahal as a tribute to her. When the emperor died many years later he was buried there too, next to his wife.

THE GREAT PYRAMID, GIZA, EGYPT

One of the seven wonders of the ancient world, this pyramid was built around 2560 B.C.! It was ordered to be built by Pharaoh Khufu as a final resting place for him. For over 3,800 years the pyramid kept the title of tallest man-made structure in the world.

FORGING AHEAD

INVENTIONS AIDING ARCHAEOLOGISTS

better view

DRONE FOOTAGE

is becoming an important addition to dig sites to **spot unusual features in the ground.**

VIRTUAL REALITY creates new ways to visit archaeological sites. Using a **VR headset** people can **walk around ancient cities.** Some museums, such as the Natural History Museum in London, are creating their exhibits in VR too. Soon you'll be able to **visit many museums from the comfort of your own home.**

visiting the past

Pooh Sticks

Some archaeologists are using chemistry to test soil for **ANCIENT HUMAN POO!** Human faeces can be detected for more than a thousand years, so can be a **good way to find vanished settlements.**

look before digging

Before archaeologists get their shovels out, they can use **GROUND-PENETRATING RADAR** to make sure they dig in the right place. This radar bounces radio waves to find out if there is something buried underneath. It can't tell them what will be down there, but it might just help them find something!

touching history

Making **3D MODELS** of ancient artefacts can allow people to touch the past without damaging the original. Even ruins that have been lost or destroyed could be saved for future visitors.

IN ICE CONDITION

Forget the ancient bag of peas in your parents' freezer, **ice can preserve creatures that have died 10,000 years ago!** Here are some of the oldest.

What you looking at?

Ötzi the Iceman is a **5,300-year-old man** found frozen in the Austrian Alps in **1991.** He was covered in about **50 tattoos.** Researchers found that he has at least **19** genetic relatives living in **Austria.**

That's a long family tree! >>>

WOOLLY RHINOCEROS (RHINO)

Woolly rhinos were one of the most abundant of **Europe's large mammals,** but very few remains have been found. In 2007 some miners in **Russia** found a well-preserved woolly rhino **frozen in the permafrost.** It is around **39,000 years old,** and had thick brown fur to help with the cold.

all horn

ice baby

LYUBA

The most complete body of a **woolly mammoth** ever discovered. The **one-month-old baby** was found by reindeer herders beside a river in **Siberia.** She is almost perfectly intact, even down to her eyelashes. She was called **Lyuba** after the wife of the man who discovered her. Scientists also believe that her discovery might one day make it possible to **clone a woolly mammoth,** bringing the species back from the dead.

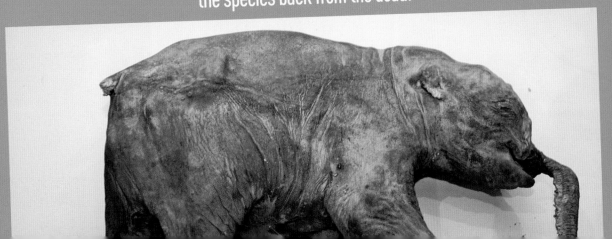

No sign of Wittenoom anymore!

Munjina 67

Wittenoom

WHERE IS IT?
Australia

HOW MANY PEOPLE USED TO LIVE THERE?
500

WHEN DID THEY LEAVE?
1966

WHY DID THEY GO?
The town was a mine for asbestos, later found to be highly dangerous.

PEOPLE USED TO LIVE HERE

Imber

WHERE IS IT?
United Kingdom

HOW MANY PEOPLE USED TO LIVE THERE?
150

WHEN DID THEY LEAVE?
1943

WHY DID THEY GO?
The town was used as a training ground during WWII.

Bodie

WHERE IS IT?
United States

HOW MANY PEOPLE USED TO LIVE THERE?
10,000

WHEN DID THEY LEAVE?
1942

WHY DID THEY GO?
Bodie was a gold mining town, but eventually the gold ran out.

Pripyat

WHERE IS IT?
Ukraine

HOW MANY PEOPLE USED TO LIVE THERE?
50,000

WHEN DID THEY LEAVE?
1986

WHY DID THEY GO?
An explosion at the nearby Chernobyl nuclear power plant caused widespread contamination.

Plymouth

WHERE IS IT?
Montserrat

HOW MANY PEOPLE USED TO LIVE THERE?
4,000

WHEN DID THEY LEAVE?
Gradually, between 1995 and 1997.

WHY DID THEY GO?
Volcanic eruption covered the whole southern part of the island.

BURIED FOR FUTURE GENERATIONS

The **Crypt of Civilization,** sealed in **1940,** contains voice recordings of people like **Franklin Roosevelt,** but also of the cartoon character **Popeye the Sailor.** The Crypt of Civilization also holds **dental floss, a Donald Duck toy,** an **electric toaster,** and many other objects.

A time capsule from the **1890s** in **Kingussie, Scotland,** was **discovered in 2015** and contained a **newspaper** and a paper scroll. It was also believed to contain a **bottle of whisky.**

In **1992, Nickelodeon** buried a time capsule containing, among other things, a **Nintendo Game Boy, a jar of Gak, Twinkies,** and a stick of **bubble gum.**

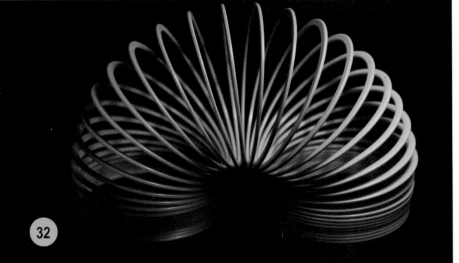

In **1970, Panasonic** constructed a capsule in **Osaka, Japan,** which contains **thousands of objects,** including a **Slinky** and the **fingernail** of a survivor of the **1945 Hiroshima bombing.**

A **Blue Peter time capsule** buried in 1998 was **accidentally dug up** in 2017 – **33 years earlier** than planned. It included **Tellytubby dolls,** a **Tamagotchi,** and an **asthma inhaler,** among other things.

Andy Warhol put 300,000 of his everyday possessions into **610 cardboard boxes,** including **letters** and **postcards** to a **lump of concrete, toenail clippings,** and **dead ants.**

Under the **Tower Bridge's** Walk of Fame is a **time capsule buried in 2017** which contains notes and objects representing people's connection to London. **Forty submissions** have been chosen and buried beneath the **40th decorative plaque** to be **unearthed** during conservation works in **40 years time.**

Harold Keith Davisson buried an entire **Chevy Vega** in **Seward, Nebraska** in **1975.** This is the **world's largest time capsule.**

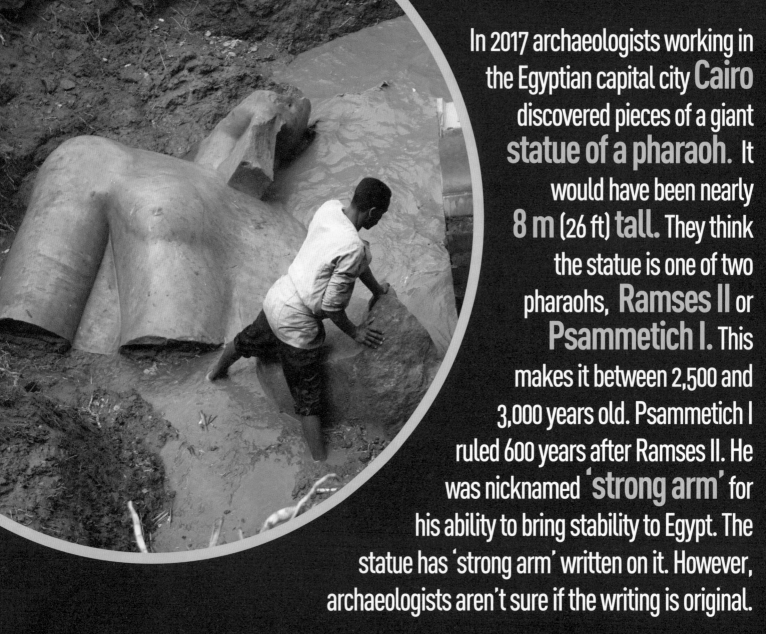

In 2017 archaeologists working in the Egyptian capital city **Cairo** discovered pieces of a giant statue of a pharaoh. It would have been nearly **8 m (26 ft) tall**. They think the statue is one of two pharaohs, **Ramses II** or **Psammetich I**. This makes it between 2,500 and 3,000 years old. Psammetich I ruled 600 years after Ramses II. He was nicknamed 'strong arm' for his ability to bring stability to Egypt. The statue has 'strong arm' written on it. However, archaeologists aren't sure if the writing is original.

BODY DOUBLE
STRIKING STATUES

WHAT IS THE TALLEST STATUE IN THE WORLD?

The tallest statue in the world is the SPRING TEMPLE BUDDHA in CHINA.

The statue was built on top of a **Buddhist** monastery and was reported to have used 1,000 tonnes (980 tons) of copper to build.

The statue itself is 128 m (420 ft) tall from top to bottom. When added to its pedestal, it towers at 208 m (682 ft) – 115 m (377 ft) taller than the Statue of Liberty.

That's one big toenail to clip.

GOING FOR GOLD

ANDREW WHELAN made one of Britain's most valuable finds in 2007. While metal detecting, he found 617 silver coins and lots of other silver items. These were eventually bought by a museum for £1 million!

>>>

Builders in 1966 accidentally found 1,237 gold coins. The hoard was thought to have been hidden by someone fleeing a battle in the War of the Roses.

<<<

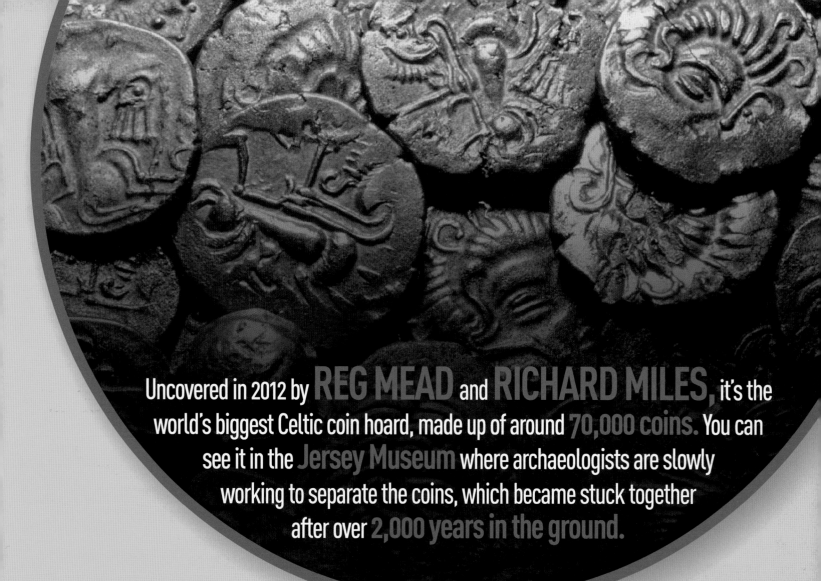

Uncovered in 2012 by **REG MEAD** and **RICHARD MILES,** it's the world's biggest Celtic coin hoard, made up of around **70,000 coins.** You can see it in the **Jersey Museum** where archaeologists are slowly working to separate the coins, which became stuck together after over **2,000 years in the ground.**

<<<

In 2012, 13-year-old **JANSEN LYONS** used a **homemade metal detector** to uncover a **two-pound meteorite.** Jansen has kept his meteorite, but gave part of it to a museum.

MISSING MAJESTIES

Where are the misplaced monarchs?

Harold II

The **last Anglo-Saxon king of England**, Harold Godwinson died at the **Battle of Hastings in 1066.** He is one of the most famous kings of England, but the man who defeated him, **William the Conqueror,** didn't think so. When Harold's mother offered to buy his body for his **weight in gold,** William refused. Instead, his **body was buried in secret** on the seashore.

Genghis Khan

When Genghis Khan died he left behind one of the **largest empires in history.** He asked to be buried without any grave markings, but did ask for his **six cats to be buried with him,** so that their purrs could take him to the afterlife. An odd request!

The warriors who buried him killed anyone they saw on the way, and then killed themselves. Many expeditions have searched for the great ruler, but none have succeeded.

Cleopatra

One of the greatest of the **Egyptian pharaohs.** She was also **one of the last.** She **killed herself after hearing of the defeat** and **death** of her husband **Marc Antony** who was fighting the Romans. They were buried together somewhere near Alexandria, but **no one knows the exact location.**

Boudicca

A warrior queen of the **Iceni.** The Iceni were a **British tribe who fought the Romans and burned London to the ground.** She was eventually defeated in battle, and is said to have taken her own life. But no one knows where the battle was, or where she is buried. There are **rumours that she is under a fast-food restaurant in Birmingham,** or **under platform 10 at King's Cross station,** but the **hunt continues.**

>>>

Attila the Hun

A **fearsome ruler** whose empire covered much of **central and eastern Europe.** He fought the Romans on many occasions, and **came close to capturing Rome.** It is thought he died at his own wedding after drinking too much. **He was placed in three coffins.** One was made of gold, the second of silver, and the third of iron. **The people who built his tomb were killed so that no one would know where he was buried.**

<<<

>>>

Alfred the Great

The king who stopped the Viking conquest of the British isles **died in 899.** He was buried in an abbey near **Winchester.** This abbey was **demolished during the reign of Henry VIII,** and the graves **forgotten about.** In 1788 a prison was built on the site, and the **graves were looted** and the **bones scattered.**

Tarsiers have huge eyes and extremely long fingers. Find out more cool facts about tarsiers on page 49.

Tarsiers can leap **40 times** their body length.

CHAPTER 3

iNCReDiBle cReATuRes

ROSEATE SPOONBILLS

This bird gets its red colour from feeding on crustaceans. It moves its beak from side to side under the water to catch its prey. Spoonbill chicks are born with a normal straight bill, and as they grow up the salad-tong shape begins to appear.

SHOEBILLS

The shoebill's beak means business. Measuring up to 24 cm (9 in) long and 20 cm (8 in) wide, it is razor sharp and can decapitate large fish and even baby crocodiles!

PELICANS

Pelicans have some of the heaviest beaks of all birds, but what is most remarkable is their massive pouches below their beaks which they use to hold fish and drain the water before swallowing.

RHINOCEROS HORNBILLS

This magnificent bird has a little something to help it be heard in the rainforests of Southeast Asia. What looks like an extra bill is actually called a casque, and can amplify its calls. The casque is made from the same material as human fingernails, keratin.

>>>

JUST THE BILL, PLEASE

BIRDS WITH AMAZING BEAKS

SWORD-BILLED HUMMINGBIRDS

A sword-billed hummingbird has a beak that can be longer than its own body, and a tongue to match! Adapted to reach nectar in hard-to-reach places, this hummingbird had to come up with a new way of grooming and itching itself. Rather than using its beak like other birds, it has to make do with a good scratch from one of its feet.

ALL CREATURES
GREAT and
SMALL

MADAME BERTHE'S MOUSE LEMURS are the world's smallest primates; weighing a tiny 30 g (1 oz) and measuring only 9 cm (3.5 in) in length.

ROBOROVSKI DWARF HAMSTERS are the smallest and fastest of all dwarf hamsters. They can run over 160 km (100 mi) in one night!

BLUE WHALES have a heart the same size as a golf buggy. In fact, their heart is so huge, you would be able to crawl through the arteries!

AFRICAN ELEPHANTS

are the largest land animal in the world, towering at a whopping 4 m (13 ft) tall. A single elephant tooth can weigh as much as 4 kg (9 lb).

Despite their size, most elephants weigh less than the tongue of a blue whale.

Did you know that elephants aren't scared of mice, despite what myths suggest? They are, however, scared of ants and bees! Some African farmers have used this to their advantage by surrounding their fields with beehives to ward off any unwelcome visitors.

CITY SCAVENGERS
ANIMALS LOOKING FOR TREATS IN TOWN

EVER SEEN A SQUIRREL PERCHED ON A LITTER BIN, OR A SEAGULL SWOOPING DOWN FOR SOME CHIPS?

City-dwelling animals on the lookout for food often seek out what humans leave behind. Junk food can be as bad for animals as it is for humans though – hopefully these animals pick healthy snacks sometimes too...

In 2017, a New York City woman spotted a squirrel tucking into a taco in a tree and uploaded a photo to Twitter. The lucky critter became an internet sensation.

Cute stripy raccoons, native to North America, are notorious trash fiends. Although they thrive in wooded habitats, an increasing number live in urban areas, and can cause damage to property in their attempts to find food. Some cities have specially designed bins specifically to stop them getting in! In Toronto, Canada, some bins have handles so they can be hung from walls to prevent raccoons from knocking them over. But in February 2017 one raccoon found itself taking a ride on a waste disposal truck when it started driving away!

'Pizza Rat' became a star after a passer-by took a video of the rodent dragging a giant slice of pizza bigger than its own body down subway stairs.

Who wouldn't want a slice of pizza so huge?

Crazy CREATURES

ECHIDNAS

These peculiar creatures are small, egg-laying mammals, with no teeth, and are covered in spines. They eat ants, worms, and larvae, which they can sniff out using an amazing sense of smell.

FUN FACT

A baby echidna is called a **puggle.**

HAIRY FROGFISH

The hairy frogfish is a hunter that walks along the seafloor instead of swimming. When it finds a good spot to hide out it sits perfectly still. Its magnificent camouflage hides it from other fish. It also has a lure which looks exactly like a worm. If a fish thinks it's in for a delicious dinner, it is very wrong indeed!

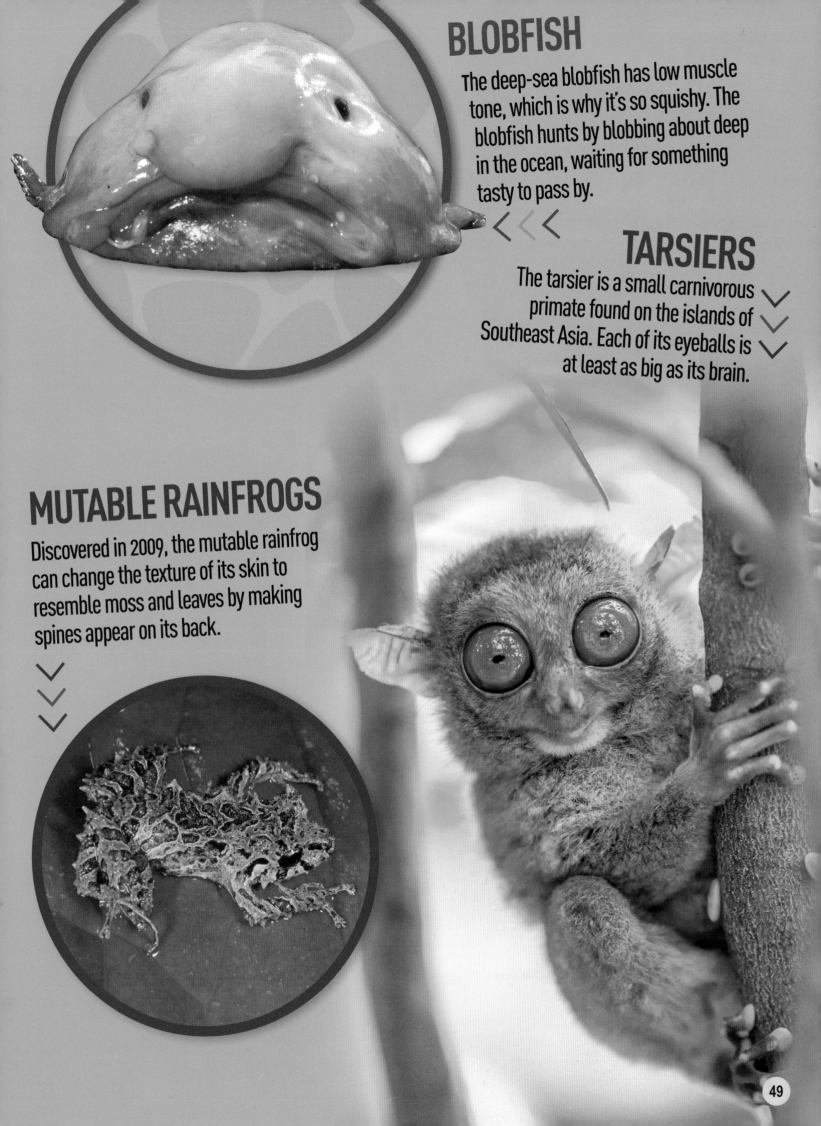

BLOBFISH

The deep-sea blobfish has low muscle tone, which is why it's so squishy. The blobfish hunts by blobbing about deep in the ocean, waiting for something tasty to pass by.

<<<

TARSIERS

The tarsier is a small carnivorous primate found on the islands of Southeast Asia. Each of its eyeballs is at least as big as its brain.

MUTABLE RAINFROGS

Discovered in 2009, the mutable rainfrog can change the texture of its skin to resemble moss and leaves by making spines appear on its back.

Living, forever?

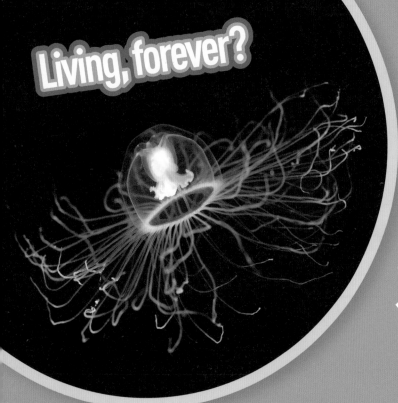

The **IMMORTAL JELLYFISH** may be able to live forever. In times of stress or injury it can age backwards, returning to its polyp form, which would be like your grandad turning back into a baby. This lets it grow old again and again and again. Seriously weird!

←

Spine tingling

In 2016 scientists found the oldest vertebrate (an animal with a spine) on Earth – a **GREENLAND SHARK**. It was around 400 years old, meaning it was born before we had discovered gravity!

→

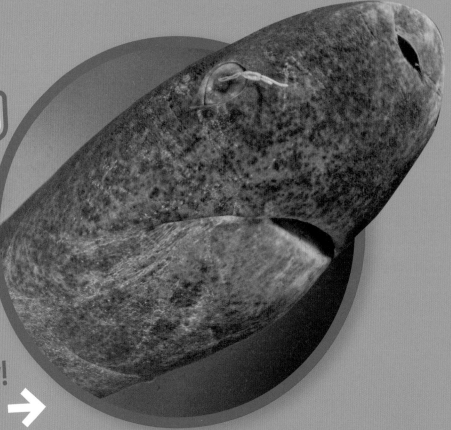

Narrow escape

A **BOWHEAD WHALE** was found with a harpoon stuck in her blubber. She must have had a lucky escape from 19th-century whale hunters. After testing her DNA it was discovered she was 211. That makes her the oldest mammal ever recorded.

←

LONG IN THE TOOTH
OLDEST LIVING ANIMALS

Go, granny, go!

HUMANS currently hold the record for **oldest land mammal**. Jeanne Louise Calment reached the grand age of 122. That's a lot of candles on a birthday cake!

Long shellf life ↑

An ocean QUAHOG called Ming was discovered to be a whopping 507 years old. Quahogs are a type of clam. Ming was found on the seabed near Iceland.

BEAVERS
are back in Britain!

After being extinct for over 400 years, there are now three large family groups – two in Scotland and one on the rather confusing river Otter in England. Beavers are a 'keystone species', which means they have many positive effects on their neighbourhood, helping other plants and animals to do well. People used to believe that beavers eat fish, but they actually eat grasses, aquatic plants, and leaves during the summer months, and in winter they eat bark and wood from young trees. They chop these down all year round using their powerful teeth and store them under their houses, called dams.

CHEEKY CHOMPERS

Those teeth are strong, but that doesn't mean they don't need looking after! Like rabbits and hamsters, beavers have to chew wood every day to stop their teeth getting too long!

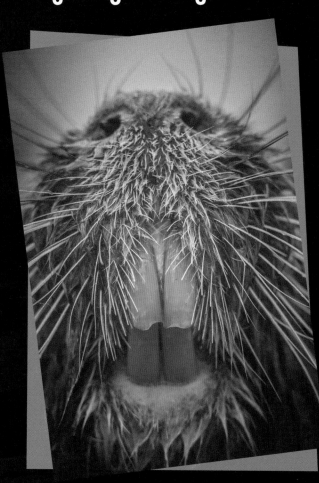

Did you know that beavers' teeth never stop growing?

YOU'VE GOAT TO BE KIDDING ME!

A British designer had a strange ambition – to live like a goat with a herd on a Swiss mountainside. He researched the project thoroughly before embarking on it, finding out what goats spend their time doing and what their behaviour was. He had special legs made in Manchester so that he could walk like a goat on all fours. One of the problems he had to overcome was that humans aren't able to eat grass, because our stomachs can't digest it. He had to come up with an alternative way of eating like a goat. His solution was to take mouthfuls of grass, chew it up, and then spit it into a bag. He would cook the chewed grass in a pressure cooker, and then feed off that throughout the day, sucking it through a straw.

GROSS!

He **lived like a goat** for **three days,** following the herd and eating grass, but found **balancing on the steep slopes** very tricky, even with his new legs! He was also a bit **scared** of the **goats' sharp horns,** as they weren't very **convinced by his behaviour.**

Man's b~~est~~ weirdest friend

STICK INSECTS
can live for **several years** and need other stick insects for company as they **dislike being alone.**

TARANTULAS
are quiet, need little space, and are easy to care for. Their bites are venomous, <u>but</u> usually no worse than **a bee or a wasp sting.**

CAPYBARAS are related to **guinea pigs** and are the **largest rodents** in the world, usually **weighing** more than **45 kg** (100 lb).

Madagascar hissing >>>
cockroaches can grow up to
7.6 cm (3 in) **long,** but they don't fly
or bite and make **great pets**.

BEARDED DRAGONS
can live between **7** and **15 years**
and shed their skin in large pieces.

 <<<

GIANT AFRICAN
LAND SNAILS are
around **18 cm** (7 in) **long.**
They are **low-maintenance**
pets that love fresh fruit and
vegetables.

 >>>

LOOK UP!

Animals that inhabit trees

SLOTHS enjoy → hanging around so much that they can retain their grip after death.

ORANGUTANS only hang out in the trees of two islands – Borneo and Sumatra in Southeast Asia. In Malay, orangutan translates to 'person of the forest'.

KOALAS love eucalyptus trees. Their diet consists almost entirely of eucalyptus leaves, which can make them smell like cough medicine! Bizarrely, koalas spend 18 hours of the day sleeping or resting.

RED-EYED TREE FROGS use suction cups on their feet to aid climbing. They are brightly coloured and have large eyes. If disturbed, these frogs abruptly reveal their eyes to startle any predators, before darting off.

GREEN TREE PYTHONS wrap themselves in coils around branches with their head resting in the centre. This anchors them in position, ready to snatch any prey below, before constricting it in the coils and then eating it whole.

Eijiro Miyako invented a drone that gives bees a helping hand. See page 75 to find out how.

Honeybees have to visit around **two million flowers** to make half a kilo of honey.

CHAPTER 4

BRIGHT IDEAS

MORE THAN HUMAN?
Modifying the human body

These people have all added parts to their bodies to replace something that is missing, like an arm, or to add something new.

Listen up

Artist **Stelios Arcadiou** has a third ear... on his arm! It isn't for him to listen with, though. He plans to put a **small microphone** in this new ear, so that anyone can listen in online.

<<<

Holding the future

In 2006 **Claudia Mitchell** became the first woman to be fitted with a **robotic arm**. She uses **her mind** to move it and grab.

<<<

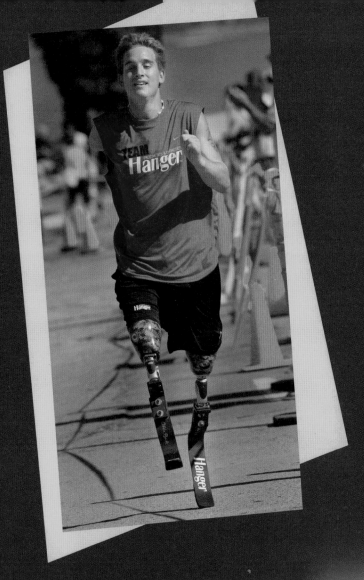

Going for gold

<<<

Cameron Clapp lost both legs as a teenager. That hasn't stopped him from winning gold medals though. With his robotic legs he can run 100 metres (328 ft) in only 18 seconds!

White noise

Artist **Neil Harbisson** was the first person to be officially named a cyborg. He has very bad colour blindness which means he can only see in black and white. He has solved this by putting a computer on his head that changes colours to sound. He uses those sounds to 'hear' colours. His favourite sound-colour is infared.

>>

CROWD-FUNDING

CROWD-FUNDING can be a great way for smart-thinking entrepreneurs to get a project off the ground. Using websites such as Kickstarter, customers who are interested in a new product or idea can pay money towards it at an early stage, a bit like a pre-order, meaning the creators know it'll be a financial success. From fashion to books, new technology to cuddly toys, all kinds of things have been started by crowd-funding.

In 2014, a man named Zach >>> 'Danger' Brown even advertised his potato salad-making services! Backers in the U.S.A. could pay $3 for a bite of potato salad, $10 to hang out in his kitchen while he made it, or $35 for a t-shirt and $50 for a recipe book. In the end, a whopping 6,911 backers raised a total of $55,492 – all for making potato salad!

UH OH!

Sometimes crowd-funders don't hit their target. Unsuccessful ideas include a **sauce-bottle satchel,** an **anti-gravity device,** and a campaign to raise enough money to **buy** crowd-funding site Kickstarter itself.

In 2012, a group of researchers crowd-funded an official squirrel census in Georgia, U.S.A., counting all the squirrels in Inman Park.

Someone once successfully raised enough money via crowd-funding to hire a skywriter plane to create silly messages in the air. One of the more notable messages was 'How do I land?' Gulp!

The grilled cheesus is a sandwich toaster which imprints the face of Jesus onto toasted bread. It might sound crazy, but this invention successfully met its funding goal and became a reality in 2012.

HOT wheels

Inventions for our furry, feathered, and fishy friends!

Some clever animal lovers have devised ingenious inventions to help their furry (or fishy!) friends out when they're in need.

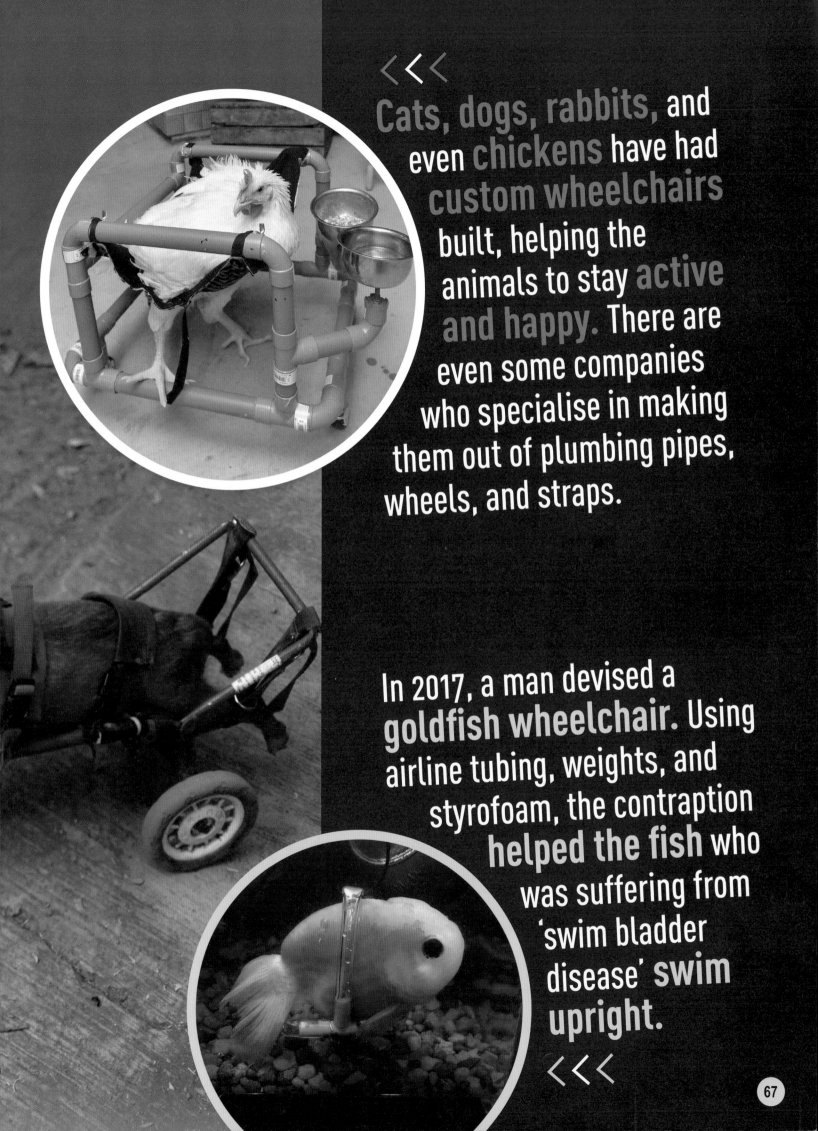

<<<

Cats, dogs, rabbits, and even chickens have had custom wheelchairs built, helping the animals to stay active and happy. There are even some companies who specialise in making them out of plumbing pipes, wheels, and straps.

In 2017, a man devised a goldfish wheelchair. Using airline tubing, weights, and styrofoam, the contraption helped the fish who was suffering from 'swim bladder disease' swim upright.

<<<

Bright sparks

Some inventors start young!

Alexander Graham Bell **started working on speech transmission when he was 18,** George Nissen **thought up the trampoline at 16,** Louis Braille **invented the touch type at 15, and** Margaret Knight **came up with the bright idea of a safety device to stop textile machinery quickly when she was only 12.**

Barack Obama **helped test** 14-year-old Joey Hudy's Extreme Marshmallow Cannon, **shooting a marshmallow across the** State Dining Room **at the** White House **during a science fair in 2012.**

Mallory Kievman

Fed up with suffering from hiccups, Kievman invented the 'Hiccupop' when she was 13 to help cure herself and others. The Hiccupop is a combination of the three things most likely to stop hiccups: apple cider vinegar, sugar, and a lollipop.

William Kamkwamba

When Kamkwamba was 15 he built a wind turbine using scrap metal, bicycle parts, and wood to power his house in Malawi. Since then he has gone on to invent a solar-powered water pump, and has built several other wind turbines in the country.

Kiara Nirghin

Here's an inventor to keep an eye on. Kiara Nirghin (16) won the 2016 grand prize at the Google Science Fair for an invention that might bring relief to countries experiencing drought. Her invention uses orange and avocado peel to create a mixture that helps soil keep hold of water.

3D PRINTING
A FACTORY IN EVERY HOME

A 3D printer can turn computer models into solid structures. Scientists believe that 3D printers will be able to produce everything from **clothes to medicines, and even food.** They can even **build themselves!** With a basic 3D printer it is possible to make new parts that can upgrade it, so you might never need to buy a new model. The models are built in a series of layers, **0.1 mm thin.** A material is heated until it is in a **semi-liquid state.** It is put where it is needed and hardens quickly. The technology is advancing rapidly and different methods are invented all the time.

Fun**FACT**

In 2017 a whole house was printed in Russia. It took just 24 hours, and used a mobile 3D printer to make the walls out of a concrete mixture. The painting still had to be done by hand though!

In the future it is likely that **every home will have a 3D printer** Rather than shopping online and then waiting for delivery, you will **buy the digital model** and **then print it.**

Printing pancakes

Students in Shenzhen, China, enjoy an exhibition showcasing 3D printed-pancakes. Batter is dispensed onto a hot griddle below and voilà, edible pancakes are prepared. The fun doesn't stop there; users can upload designs to the machine via an SD card to create their own picture-perfect pancake.

Helping hand

Belarusian engineer Sergei Galstev created an artificial limb for his dad using parts created by 3D printing. That really is handy!

Making music

Violinist Eva Rabchevska performs at the '3D Printing the World' exhibition using a printed violin. What instrument would you like to print?

Talking RUBBISH
CLEANING THE OCEANS

There are an estimated 5.25 trillion pieces of plastic floating in our oceans. Cleaning this up is becoming a necessity. This is because the plastic is deadly for birds and sea life. Also a lot of it ends up on our beaches and harbours, making them very polluted.

Two Australian surfers, Peter Ceglinski and Andrew Turton, think they have the solution. Called the SEABIN, it could prove to be one of the most important inventions of the century.

Seabin

The Seabin is a cylinder that floats just below the surface of the water. A pump at the bottom draws water through the cylinder. This water moves through a filter made of natural materials. The filter traps all the rubbish that was floating on top of the sea, but allows eggs and small sea creatures to pass through. At first, the Seabins are only going to be used in ports and marinas. This is because the Seabins will need to be emptied regularly, and harbours are more sheltered than the open ocean. The first port to trial the Seabin in 2017 will be Portsmouth in the UK.

tastes like chicken

ARTIFICIAL MEAT is being developed by a number of companies around the world. They see it as a way to **REDUCE THE CARBON FOOTPRINT** of farming. It might also help **FEED THE EARTH'S GROWING POPULATION.** In 2017 an American company served up **LAB-GROWN SOUTHERN-FRIED CHICKEN.** Apparently it looks and tastes just like the real thing. A survey of Americans showed that 31% would definitely be willing to try lab-grown meat and 34% said that they would probably try it. Would you?

breathing easy

A student at the Royal College of Art, Julian Melchiorri, has created an **ARTIFICIAL LEAF** by combining plant cells and silk. The leaf absorbs water and carbon dioxide and produces oxygen, just like a real plant. But it is much stronger and **CAN COPE WITH EXTREME SITUATIONS.** Julian believes that they could be **USED ON LONG SPACE JOURNEYS TO KEEP ASTRONAUTS BREATHING.**

ARTIFICIAL AGE
MANUFACTURING NATURE

A sting in the tail

Scientists are becoming increasingly worried about **bees dying out.** Bees and other insects **pollinate** around **three quarters of all crops,** but they are in trouble from dangers such as **diseases, pesticides,** and **climate change.** Scientist **Eijiro Miyako** is developing a **drone** that can do the **job of a bee.** His tiny robot may not look like a bee, but it has a strip of **sticky hairs** that can **collect pollen** and take it to another **flower.**

FLIP SIDE

THIS IS THE UNDERSIDE OF THE DRONE – YOU CAN SEE THE STRIP OF STICKY HAIRS THAT COLLECTS POLLEN.

Researchers have found a way to grow human skin in a laboratory. It is the most life-like skin grown so far. They hope it will stop testing products on animals.

METAL MINDS
REVOLUTIONARY ROBOTS

Travelling to Singapore? Look out for robots when you pass through the new Terminal 4 at Changi Airport.

Robotic cleaners will help keep the airport spick and span with little need of human intervention. Unfortunately they can't help you tidy your bedroom! Cutting edge technology, such as face-recognition software and automated bag-tagging, will also be used to assist travellers on their journeys.

FAST FOOD? COMING RIGHT UP!

At a pizzeria in Multan, Pakistan, your meal is served by a robotic waitress. Not only can the robots navigate through the restaurant to the diner's table, they can greet the customer, negotiate obstacles, and make their way back to the kitchen. The only problem is, how much do you tip?

YOU'RE UNDER ROBOTIC ARREST

The first operational police robot in the world can be found in Dubai, U.A.E. It won't be the last robotic officer to be deployed either; the Dubai police force aim to make 25% of their officers robotic by 2030.

La Tête Carrée was designed by Sacha Sosno, a French sculptor. Find out more about this unique building on page 87.

La Tête Carrée, which literally means 'The Square Head', is a library in Nice, France.

MiNDboGGliNg buildINgs

Great Pyramid of Giza

Where: Giza, egypt
Built: 2540 B.C.
Height: 139 m (456 ft); originally 146 m (481 ft)
Length of record: 4,000 years. It took 40,000 people around 20 years to build this tomb.

Where: Lincoln, UK
Built: 1311
Height: 160 m (520 ft)
Length of record: 238 years
The cathedral lost its record when a storm blew the spire down in 1549.

Lincoln Cathedral

Eiffel Tower

Where: Paris, France
Built: 1889
Height: 324 m (1,063 ft)
Length of record: 41 years
The tower was meant to be a temporary exhibit and was nearly torn down in 1909.

Chrysler Building

Where: New York, U.S.A.
Built: 1930
Height: 319 m (1,047 ft)
Length of record: 11 months
This art deco skyscraper was built at a rate of four floors a week.

TALLEST STRUCTURES

Empire State Building

Where: New york, U.S.A.
Built: 1931
Height: 381 m (1,250 ft)
Length of record: 36 years
The record for running up its 1,576 stairs is 9 minutes 33 seconds. This was the first building to have more than 100 floors.

Ostankino Tower

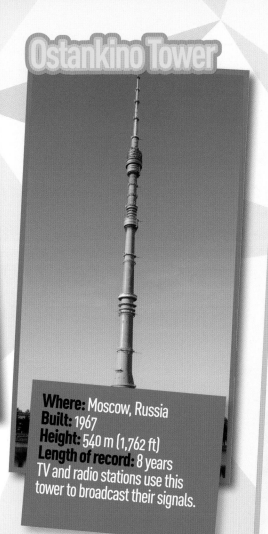

Where: Moscow, Russia
Built: 1967
Height: 540 m (1,762 ft)
Length of record: 8 years
TV and radio stations use this tower to broadcast their signals.

Jeddah Tower

Where: Jeddah, Saudi Arabia
Built: 2020 (estimate)
Height: 1,008 m (3,307 ft)
Length of record: ?
This will be the first building to stand more than one kilometre tall.

CN Tower

Where: Toronto, Canada
Built: 1975
Height: 553 m (1,815 ft)
Length of record: 34 years
Would you dare to take the Edge Walk around the outside of the tower, 356 m (1,168 ft) above the street?

Burj Khalifa

Where: Dubai, U.A.E.
Built: 2010
Height: 830 m (2,700 ft)
Length of record: 2010 to present (current record holder)
This added an eiffel tower to the world record.

HOLDING TIGHT

A 'spite house' is a building built for the purpose of annoying someone else. Sometimes it's because of a dispute over land, or when a homeowner refuses to suit surrounding buildings.

The **skinny house** in the north end of **Boston, Massachusetts,** is a four-storey building reported as having the 'uncontested distinction of being the narrowest house in Boston'.

Legend has it that two brothers inherited a plot of land from their father. While one of the brothers was away on military duty, the other built a large house on the plot, leaving only a tiny piece of land unsuitable to build on – or so he thought! When the soldier got back and found out what his brother had done, he built the narrow house out of spite, blocking sunlight and ruining his brother's view!

When **Edith Macefield's** Seattle house was in the middle of a proposed new shopping mall, **developers offered** her **one million dollars** to move. **She turned it down!**

In **China,** homes with **owners who refuse to move** for new developments springing up around them are called **nail houses.**

Unusual Schools

THE SCHOOL RUN THAT'S SUPER FUN

Daisy is nine years old and is heading to school – on a zip line at 64 km/h (40 mph)! Her remote village is on one side of the Rio Negro river in Colombia, and her school is on the other. She controls her speed on the crossing using the wooden fork. And guess what's in that grey bag? It's her five-year-old brother, Jamid – he's too young to make the run on his own!

Some children around the world go to school in some very unusual places – and ways.
What do you think learning here would be like?

CHILL OUT

Ørestad College in Copenhagen, Denmark has an ultra-modern building. Students go to school in a giant glass cube. Inside, there are 'drums' (like in the image) where students can relax, and some of the walls and bookshelves can even be moved to create areas for smaller study groups.

ALL ABOARD THE FLOATING SCHOOL

Bangladesh is a very low-lying country, meaning that the land isn't very high above sea level. It is criss-crossed with rivers that often flood. This makes it pretty tricky to go to school sometimes.

To overcome this, some villages have built schools that float!

BIZARRE BUILDINGS

In **Tirau, New Zealand,** there are buildings that look like a **dog,** a **sheep,** and a **ram.**

The **China Central Television** Headquarters in **Beijing** is 234 m (768 ft) high and has been nick-named **'big pants'** by locals.

The **Eden Project** in **Cornwall** opened in 2001 and contains plants from many diverse climates and environments. It is home to the **world's largest indoor rainforest** and boasts nearly **5,000 varieties of plants** – the stinkiest being the dragon arum, which smells of rotten flesh! **England's longest** and **fastest zip line** can also be found here.

Are you brave enough to zip over 660 m (2,200 ft) at speeds of up to 97 km/h (60 mph)?

La Tête Carrée library in **Nice**, France, is 26 m (85 ft) high and holds **three floors of books.**

The **Cube Houses** in **Rotterdam,** The Netherlands, were opened in 1977 and based on the concept of **'living as an urban roof'.**

SAGRADA FAMÍLIA

There's no other building quite like the Sagrada Família in Barcelona, Spain.

Work on the church **started in 1882,** but it **won't be finished until 2026.** It is taking a long time because the architect, **Antoni Gaudí,** created a design that is very big and **very ornate.** The Sagrada Família will have a total of **18 spires.** One will be **170 m** (560 ft) **high,** making this the **tallest church in the world.** It has three large facades that are all packed with very **intricate carvings.** In the nave the columns that support the roof twist and **branch out like living trees.**

aerial view

ornate detail

stained-glass windows

main altar

interior ceiling

BUILDING →

Totally tulips! The Aalsmeer Flower Auction in the Netherlands covers more ground than any other building in the world. It is 740 m (2,400 ft) long and 700 m (2,300 ft) broad – that means you could fit 74 football pitches inside!

← STATION

Trainspotters must visit Grand Central Terminal in New York City at least once in their lives. It covers 190,000 square metres (47 acres) and has 44 platforms – more than any other railway station in the world. It's also very beautiful!

AMUSEMENT PARK →

The Magic Kingdom in Florida is the world's biggest amusement park, with 20,492,000 fun-lovers coming to enjoy the rides in 2015. Walt Disney World Resort is the world's largest entertainment complex and covers 110 km^2 (40 sq mi).

← CLOCK

Found at the top of the world's third-highest place is the world's largest and highest clock. The clock faces on the Makkah Royal Clock Tower in Mecca, Saudi Arabia, are 530 m (1,300 ft) above the ground and are 43 m (140 ft) across.

HOTEL →

Talk about a lot of towels – the First World Hotel in Pahang, Malaysia, is the largest hotel in the world with 7,351 rooms.

BIGGEST

RESTAURANT

More people sit down to dinner at the Damascus Gate Restaurant in Damascus, Syria, than in any other restaurant in the world. There are 6,014 seats spread over 54,000 square metres (13 acres). In peak season, up to 1,800 staff are employed.

SCHOOL

The City Montessori School in Lucknow, India, is the world's biggest school. It has over 1000 classrooms and over 50,000 students! Breaktime must get pretty crazy...

CHURCH

You could easily fit two football pitches inside St Peter's Basilica in Rome, Italy. Its dome is the tallest in the world at 136.6 m (448 ft) and it was designed by the famous Renaissance artist Michelangelo.

LIBRARY

Washington D.C.'s Library of Congress is home to over 164 million items on around 1,350 km (838 mi) of bookshelves, making it the biggest library in the world.

MUSEUM

More people visit the Louvre in Paris, France, than any other museum. Over 7.4 million people popped by in 2016 to marvel at 38,000 objects including the Mona Lisa.

What gadgets and gizmos would you like in your Smart Home? Why not get some paper and design your future house today?

WHERE WILL YOU LIVE IN THE FUTURE?

IMAGINE IF YOUR HOUSE WAS SMART.

Like it could automatically turn the lights off when the sun is shining. Or send you a message to let you know that you've left your console on. It would have see-through solar panels for windows so you would never need to worry about your electricity bill. It would collect its own water by harvesting the rain, and even the paint on the walls would be special – it would act as an insulator to keep heat in.

Well, such a house already exists. A Smart Home at the Building Research Establishment in Watford has been fitted with the latest energy-saving features. The Smart Home is intelligent; constantly checking its sensors to adjust the heating, lighting, ventilation, water, and security. There are solar panels in the windows and the plaster on the walls has special insulating powers. No wonder the Smart Home earns top marks for energy efficiency. It even has a remote control electronic key!

WHAT GOES UP...

These demolitions look like a scene form a disaster movie but don't be alarmed! **As the demolitions are controlled, nobody gets hurt!**

In 2016, the tallest concrete structure in Britain was demolished in a spectacular controlled explosion. The towering chimney on the Isle of Grain was 2.5 times taller than Big Ben – that's higher than 55 double-decker buses stacked on top of each other! The chimney was part of an old power station that closed in 2012.

Leaning towers of Glasgow

Sometimes demolitions don't go so smoothly. Glasgow's Red Road flats were the tallest residential buildings in Europe when they were built in the 1960s, but by 2015 they were in poor condition. Six of the tower blocks were rigged with explosives ready to be demolished, but two blocks didn't fall down as planned, leaving them teetering precariously.

First floor: Telephones, gents, shirts, suits, ties, hats. Going down...

The largest building to be brought down by controlled demolition was the **Hudson Department Store** in Detroit, U.S.A., in **1998**. It was **134 m (440 ft) tall.**

STRANGE SLEEPOVERS

UNUSUAL HOTELS FROM AROUND THE GLOBE

Ever fancied having breakfast with a giraffe? Or bunking in a room made of ice? Perhaps snoozing in an aeroplane in the jungle is more your thing? Don't worry, these wonderful hotels have you covered!

The world's first ICE HOTEL opened in Jukkasjärvi, Sweden. The hotel, and even the chairs and beds, are made from snow and ice! The old hotel had to be rebuilt every year, between December and April, but a more recent one is constantly kept at sub-zero temperatures so is open to the public all year round.

Chilly check-in

Jungle slumber

No need to panic, this vintage Boeing 727 is supposed to be there. The **HOTEL COSTA VERDE** in the Manuel Antonio National Park in Costa Rica has a suite housed in the aircraft shell. You need a head for heights though, this structure juts out 15 m (50 ft) into the jungle canopy!

Breakfast buddies

GIRAFFE MANOR

in Nairobi, Kenya, is home to a tower of Rothschild's giraffes. Expect to share your breakfast – the giraffes are renowned for poking their heads through the hotel windows in search of treats!

Take a look at page 107 for why people in Madeira get around by toboggan.

The **longest** toboggan run in Europe is in **Switzerland**. It's **15 km (9 mi)**, with a vertical drop of **1,600 m (5,200 ft)**.

6

geT a MoVE ON!

Off the rails

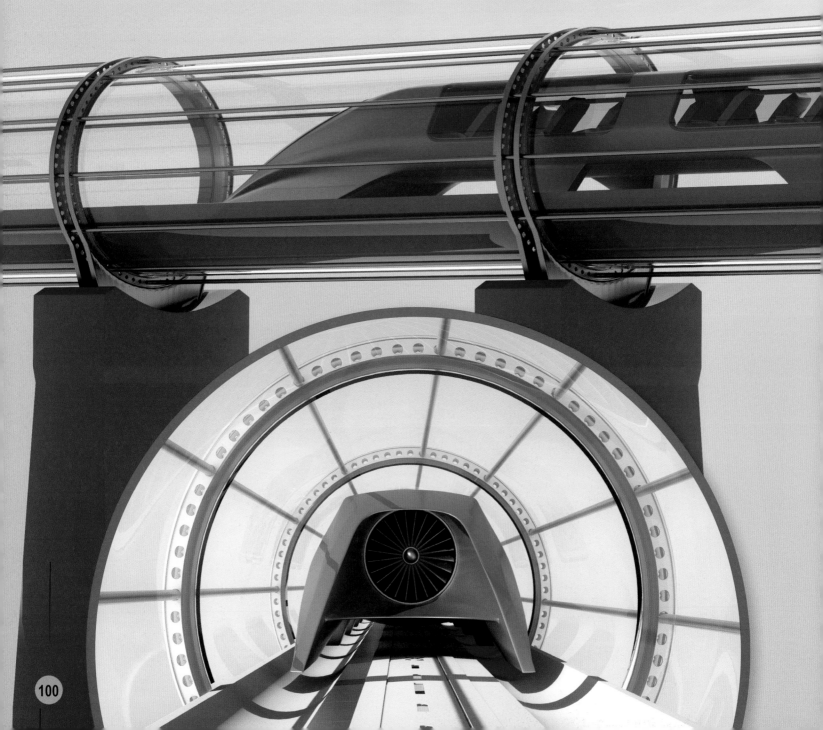

In 2017, a **500 m** (1,600 ft) **test track** was built near **Las Vegas** by a company called **Hyperloop One**. **Slovakia** is looking at building a hyperloop to **connect the cities** of **Vienna, Bratislava,** and **Budapest.**

A **hyperloop** is a **small carriage** that **travels through** **a tube** surrounded by a **pocket of air.**

GOING SOLO

ONE MAN'S RECORD-BREAKING SAILING TRIP

THOMAS COVILLE, 48, beat the **RECORD FOR SAILING AROUND THE WORLD SOLO. He** did it in **49 DAYS AND 3 HOURS,** beating the record by **8 days.**

He **rarely slept** for more than **30 minutes** at a time.

Coville's **trimaran** was **31 m** (102 ft) **long** and **21 m** (69 ft) **wide.**

To beat the record, Thomas had to travel a **total distance of 52,000 km** (32,000 mi).

PETS ON PLANES

Did you know that **falcons** are the **national bird** of the **United Arab Emirates**? **Falconry** is a **popular sport**. The birds are **frequently transported** by **plane**. In **2017**, a **whole plane-load** of the birds **went on a trip!**

PET RELIEF

Some airports have **special pet relief stations** next to bathrooms! **Airlines have different policies** about **animals on planes,** whether they're pets or hard-working **assistance dogs.** Small pets are often kept in carriers, but sometimes dogs are **allowed their own seat** – lucky ones get the window view.

PET PASSPORT

European Union
UNITED KINGDOM

Fancy taking your **pooch to Paris** or your **kitty to Krakow?** Or perhaps taking your **ferret to Florence?** Did you know **pets can travel on holiday** with you?

Make sure you get a pet passport before you go!

Not many forms of transport have survived almost unchanged for over 3,000 years, but the caballitos de totora have. These are boats made from reeds, used to catch fish in Peru. The fishermen ride the boat like a horse (caballito is Spanish for 'little horse') when out at sea, but when returning to shore, they stand on top as if the boats are a surfboard.

When you want to get around Canada's Columbia icefield a taxi simply won't cut the mustard. A weird combination of monster truck and school bus, the Terra Bus is designed to carry up to 56 people over the roughest terrain on those huge tyres. At nearly 4 m (13 ft) tall, passengers are promised a good view!

China has one of the most advanced railways in the world – a maglev. Maglev is short for magnetic levitation. It uses the power of strong magnets repelling one another to keep it above the tracks, allowing it to travel up to 431 km/h (268 mph) and to complete its 30 km (19 mi) journey in less than 8 minutes.

To get from Portsmouth to the Isle of Wight there's one way you can always travel in style – by hovercraft. Lifted above the surface of the water by a cushion of air, hovercrafts offer a smooth, fast way to travel.

On the island of Madeira, almost everything is on a slope. Keen to find a good way to get around, the locals developed a unique way to get downhill fast. They use a toboggan. The seats are wicker, the runners are wooden, and they are pushed and steered by two men wearing straw hats. The route goes from the town of Monte to the capital, Funchal, a distance of about 2 km (1.2 mi). At the end of the journey the passengers get off, and the two men haul their toboggan back up the mountain.

STRANGE TRANSPORT

BIKE BANTER
Tales of the two wheeler

What a waste of wheels

Around **13,000 bikes** are **pulled** out of **Amsterdam's canals** each **year**. That could mean an average of **36 bikes** fall into the canals **every day...**

In 1954, a **15-year-old** American boy said goodbye to his parents one morning and then **cycled 1,100 km (700 mi)** over one week from **Washington, D.C. to Atlanta.** The motivation? He was homesick for his **grandma's fried chicken!**

In America, police put **cardboard cut-outs** of **police officers** next to **bike racks.** The number of **bikes stolen** dropped by **67%.**

Peculiar Pumpkins

In 2013 **British** artist **Dmitri Galitzine** fitted a giant pumpkin with an **outboard motor**. He then **crossed the Solent**, a channel of water **almost 5 km (3 mi) wide** between the mainland of England and the Isle of Wight. It took him 1 hour and 56 minutes.

Giant pumpkins are **not very nice to eat.** Because they grow so fast and **drink so much water** they **taste very bland.**

The heaviest **pumpkin** weighed in at **1,190.49 kg (2,624.6 lb)!** and was grown by **Mathias Willemijns**.

Every autumn something remarkable happens in **Nova Scotia, Canada.** People come to **Windsor,** by **Lake Pesaquid,** to race giant pumpkins across the lake. That is a distance of **800 m** (2,600 ft), while standing in a pumpkin. There are **three classes of race: motor, experimental,** and **paddling.** The pumpkins are hollowed out and decorated. Some pumpkins are so large they can **fit two people inside them** and **can weigh over 300 kg** (660 lb). They are also very hard to steer, and tend to spin around rather than move forwards.

TAKEN FOR A RIDE
CARS WITH NO DRIVERS?

Ownership

Driverless cars look likely to be shared rather than owned. Why have a car parked for most of the day when it could be off helping someone else get from A to B?

Road congestion

A car that knows where all other cars are around them might mean the end of the traffic jam. There would be no need to stop until your destination because cars would allow each other the room to manoeuvre.

Time

Britons spend an average of 10 hours a week driving their cars. Just imagine what they could do with all that extra time. Many companies design cars that look more like a living room for ultimate comfort.

Safety

Human error causes 90% of car accidents. A driverless car will never fall asleep at the wheel, drive too fast, or get road rage. They will be more aware of their surroundings as they will have sensors all around them.

OFF THE BEATEN TRACK

Could you cope with some of the world's toughest ENDURANCE RACES?

At **only 60 km** (37 mi) the **ISLE OF MAN TT** doesn't look like a very tough race. But it takes place on **public roads** filled with telephone boxes and lampposts, at **average speeds** of up to **210 km/h** (130 mph) and there are **no crash barriers**. It is one of the **most difficult motorcycle races** in the world.

The **DAKAR RALLY** is a 15-day off-road race that covers **thousands of kilometres** and takes place over mountains and deserts. **Over 500 people compete** against each other, from **professional drivers** to **amateurs.**

Travelling **3,000 km (1,900 mi) through India** by car is an adventure in itself, but when you're travelling in India's **RICKSHAW RUN,** it takes on epic proportions! A rickshaw is a **small three-wheeled taxi** with a seven-horsepower engine, which is **slightly bigger** than a **lawnmower.**

There's more about Tim Peake's space adventures on pages 126–127.

Tim Peake was one of the six applicants chosen from 8,000 to go into space in December 2015.

CHAPTER 7

OuT of this WORLd!

TELESCOPE TRIVIA

The **HUBBLE SPACE TELESCOPE** is 13.3 m (43.5 ft) long, weighs 11 tonnes (24,000 lb) and is powered by solar panels. Hubble was key to scientific research into the age of the universe – it's thought to be a whopping 13.8 billion years old.

The first developed reflecting telescopes, like this one, were invented by Isaac Newton in 1668. Hubble is a space reflecting telescope, meaning that it works in much the same way as this smaller telescope. There's no end of things to look for in the night sky through a telescope: craters on the moon, the bands of cloud circling Jupiter, and the Big Dipper star constellation are to name but a few!

THE NEW SPACE RACE

DOING THE SAME THING AGAIN AND AGAIN IS BORING, RIGHT? NOT WHEN YOU'RE SENDING SPACECRAFTS INTO SPACE. THEN IT'S REALLY VERY COOL.

How would you like to enter a competition to design and build a moon rover to scoop a grand prize of $20 million?

Google have issued a **challenge** for private groups to do just that. Their **Lunar XPRIZE** is a challenge to **land a robotic spacecraft on the moon, travel 500 m** (1,500 ft), and send back **high-definition videos** of the adventure. Do that and you win the money!

Be the **first team** to complete the entire mission and you will bag **$20 million.** Don't worry if you finish in **second place** as you will still pocket a handsome **$5 million.**

Countries from around the globe are represented including **Japan, India, Israel,** and the **U.S.A.**

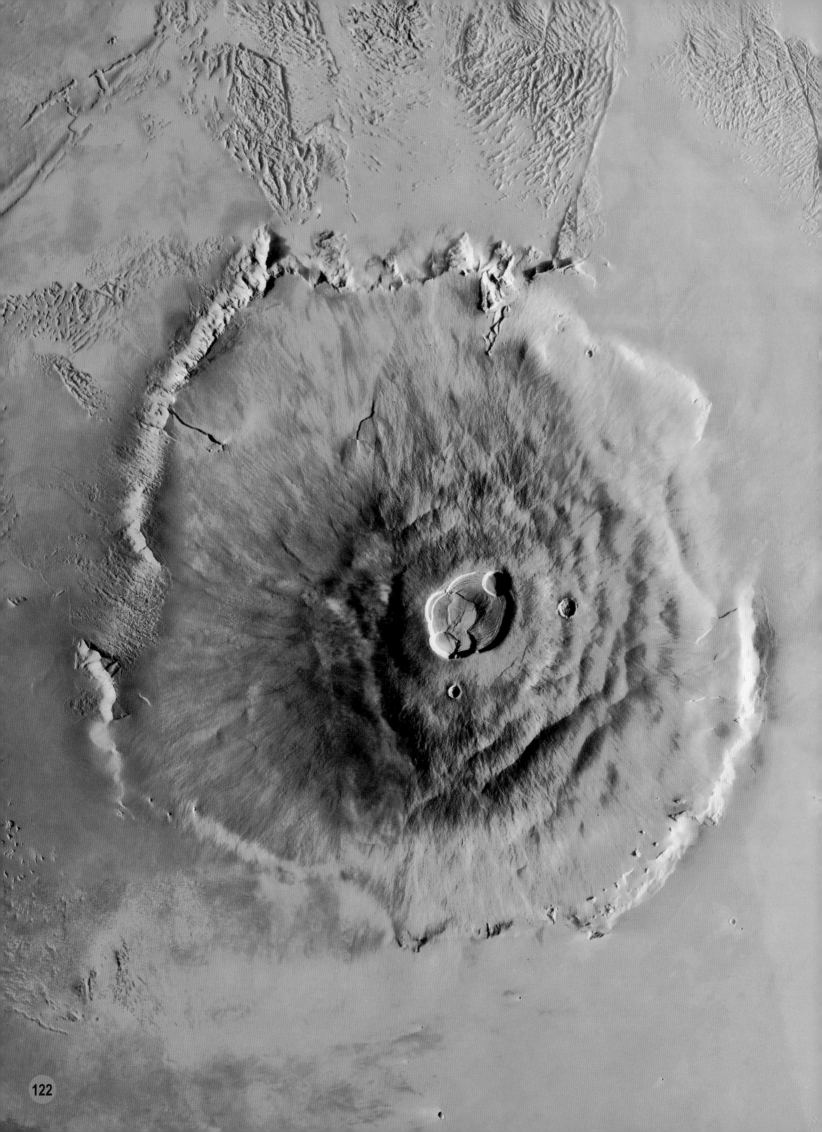

A VOLCANO BIGGER THAN EVEREST?

Of all the planets in the solar system, Mars has the largest volcano. Its name? OLYMPUS MONS.

Towering at 25 km (16 mi), Olympus Mons is almost three times the height of Mount Everest. It's not just tall either; measuring 624 km (388 mi) wide. Earth's largest volcano is Mauna Loa in Hawaii. It stands at 10 km (6.3 mi) tall and measures 120 km (75 mi) wide—tiny in comparison to Olympus Mons. In fact, Olympus Mons is so huge, its volume is 100 times the size of Mauna Loa and is big enough to fit the entire chain of Hawaiian islands from Kaui to Hawaii inside. That is BIG!

Olympus Mons in comparison to Mount Everest

THE BIG PROBLEM WITH EXPLORING SPACE IS... ITS SIZE

The **NEAREST STAR** outside our own solar system is **ALPHA CENTAURI** (a triple star system), which is **4.3 light years away.**

How far is a light year? Well, light travels at 299,792,458 m/s. That's **300,000 km** – or seven and a half circuits of the Earth – in a single second. So a light year works out at 9.4 million million km. And **our galaxy** is **100,000 light years across.** It will take a long time to explore.

ALPHA
CENTAURI

Worm holes

These are shortcuts through space from one place in the universe to another. A bit like a tube-slide in the playground – you dive in at one end and pop out somewhere else! Warp drives and worm holes are just ideas at the moment.

But who knows in future...?

Einstein also said that big objects like stars bend space. Light and other particles then curve round the bend rather than go in a straight line. This is why the Earth orbits the Sun. The creators of Star Trek came up with a 'warp drive' as a way for a spaceship to warp, or bend, space and so travel faster than light.

LIFE
IN THE
HEAVENS
Tim Peake's time in space

In December 2015, **Tim Peake** climbed aboard a **Soyuz rocket** and blasted off to spend the next **six months** of his life in a metal container **400 km** (250 mi) **above the surface of our planet.** Tim was the latest astronaut to tackle a mission on the **International Space Station.** His first meal on board his new home was a **bacon sandwich** and a **cup of tea.** While he was on board he did several experiments, completed a space walk to fix some broken equipment, and even **ran the London Marathon on a treadmill!**

Being in space **took its toll on Tim's body.** Such a long mission can **age the cardiovascular system, decrease bone density, accelerate skin ageing,** and **weaken eyesight** and **muscles.** Happily, after a few months back on Earth, Tim was pretty much **back to normal.**

(9) UNUSUAL THINGS THAT HAVE BEEN SENT INTO

AVIATOR AMELIA EARHART'S WATCH AND SCARF.

A CORNED BEEF SANDWICH IN 1965

IT FLOATED APART IN ZERO GRAVITY!

MANY SOUND RECORDINGS INCLUDING LAUGHTER, A HUMAN HEARTBEAT, RAIN FALLING, AND A TRACTOR.

THE ASHES OF JAMES DOOHAN WHO PLAYED SCOTTY IN STAR TREK.

SPACE

32 MONKEYS

NOT ALL AT THE SAME TIME!

LUKE SKYWALKER'S LIGHTSABER.

SALMONELLA BACTERIA, WHICH BECAME MUCH MORE VIRULENT.

MANY SPIDERS TO SEE IF THEY CAN MAKE WEBS IN SPACE... THEY CAN!

A PIZZA DELIVERED BY PIZZA HUT TO COSMONAUT YURI USACHOV IN 2001.

THE PARKS YOU GO TO AT NIGHT!

Natural Bridges Monument was named the world's first International Dark Sky Park in 2007.

Street lights are great for helping us get around cities at night, but they are very bad news for astronomers. All that light makes it hard to see stars! Dark Sky Parks are places far away from cities where there is no 'light pollution'.

At a Dark Sky Park you can see distant stars and galaxies just as our ancestors did, without the orange glow of street lights and neon signs.

If you are trying to see faint stars, don't look directly at them. Instead, look slightly to one side – you will be seeing with your eyes' rod cells instead of your cone cells. These are more sensitive to light and dark.

As well as stars and planets, you can get a great view of meteor showers. The best shower of the year is the Perseids, which peaks on 12 August at over one meteor per minute.

There are 11 International Dark Sky Reserves in the world, and four of them are in the UK – the Brecon Beacons, Exmoor, Snowdonia, and the South Downs National Parks.

The **Isle of Coll** in **Scotland** is **32 km (20 mi)** from the nearest lamppost, and is **one** of only **two dark sky islands.**

SEARCHING FOR ALIENS
IS THERE LIFE ON SATURN'S MOON?

In 2017, scientists announced that life could be found on Saturn's icy moon – **Enceladus.**

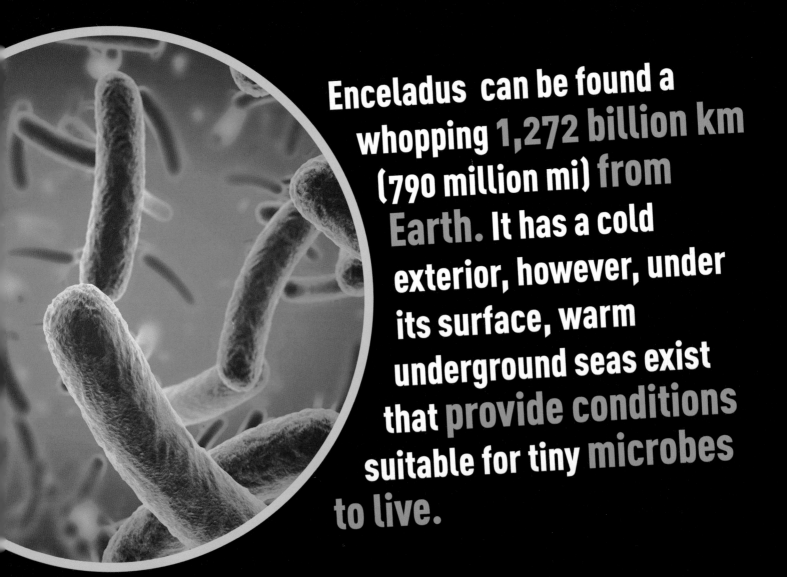

Enceladus can be found a whopping 1,272 billion km (790 million mi) from Earth. It has a cold exterior, however, under its surface, warm underground seas exist that provide conditions suitable for tiny microbes to live.

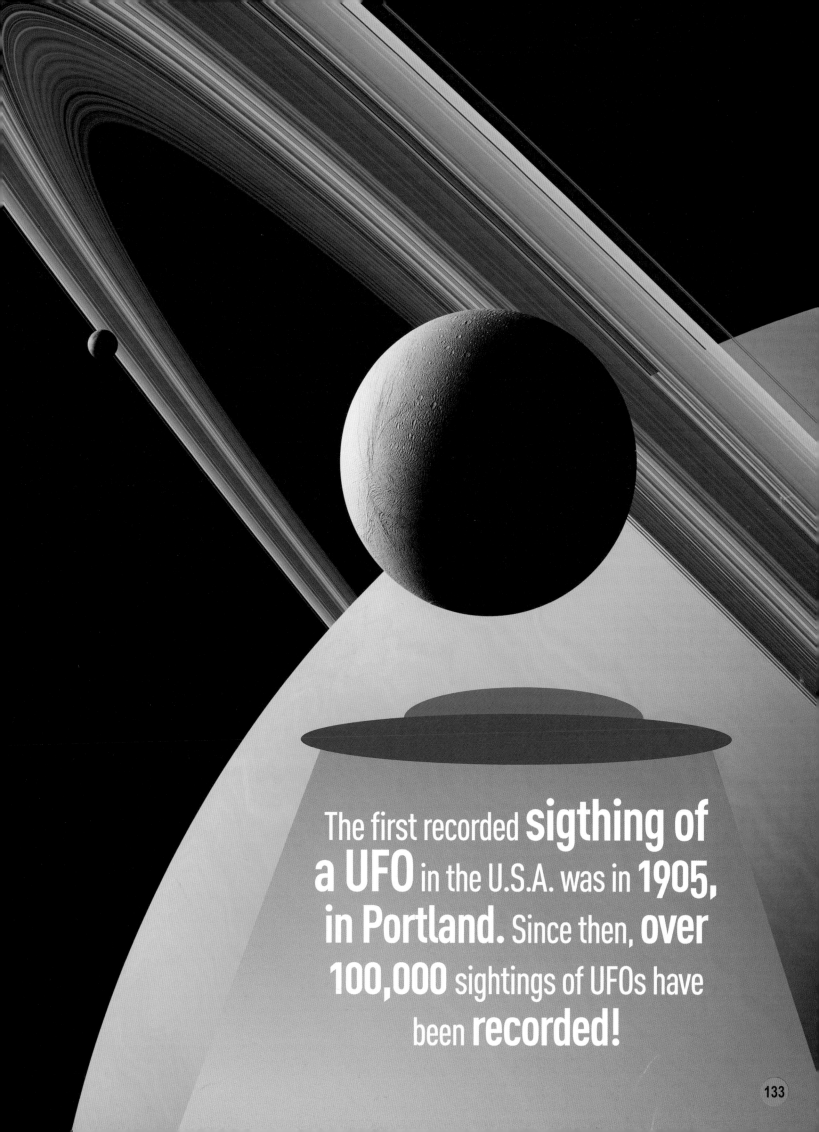

The first recorded **sigthing of a UFO** in the U.S.A. was in **1905, in Portland.** Since then, **over 100,000** sightings of UFOs have been **recorded!**

Sure you're brave enough to go on the world's fastest zip line? Check out page 146 for more information.

Zip lines weren't always just for fun — they were a means of transport across rough terrain.

SPoRTiNG SuPeRStaRS

BOG SNORKELLING

This takes place every year at the Waen Rhydd peat bog, near Llanwrtyd Wells in Mid Wales.

CHEESE ROLLING

Ever seen someone rolling a cheese down a street? Unlikely, unless you live in the English village of Stilton. This is where the famous stinky cheese is made, and where the annual Cheese Rolling World Championship happens every May.

SNAIL RACING

This isn't so much about crowning the fastest snail, as finding the one that is least slow.

You don't have to be an Olympic athlete or an elite competitor to be a champion of the world. The World Poohsticks Champion in 2016 was a seven-year-old boy called Charlie Roman. It turns out that there are hundreds of strange sports and activities that don't need strength or size to win. If you have a fast-moving younger brother or sister, they could enter the World Baby Crawling Championship. Yes, the babies line up in lanes and have to crawl as fast as possible towards the finish line. Before they start crying or fill their nappies, that is. If you have fast fingers, go for competitive Cup Stacking or Yo-Yoing. One very easy-to-practise sport is Welly Wanging – all you have to do is throw a wellington boot as far as you can. Some weird sports you can even practise in your house – Paper Plane Throwing, Pillow Fighting, or the ancient games of Marbles and Conkers. There is one strange sport that you can do in your garden, but we don't recommend it – Stinging Nettle Eating. That's not just weird, that's totally wacky.

WORLD SPEED RECORD

On Snow: 227.720 km/h (141.499 mph)

On Gravel: 172 km/h (107 mph)

KM/H - WORD SPEED RECORD
ERIC BARONE - 2017   227.720

ÉRIC BARONE HAS
THE NEED FOR SPEED!

THE **FRENCH SPORTSMAN** HOLDS THE WORLD SPEED RECORD FOR **BICYCLE** ON BOTH **GRAVEL** AND **SNOW.**

227.72 km/h

ASHIMA SHIRAISHI

ASHIMA SHIRAISHI, FROM AMERICA, IS ONE OF THE STRONGEST YOUNG CLIMBERS EVER RECORDED. SHE WAS ONLY SIX YEARS OLD WHEN SHE BEGAN TO CLIMB – IN PLACES LIKE CENTRAL PARK AND BROOKLYN BOULDERS.

MIRA RAI

MIRA RAI IS AN ULTRA-RUNNER TRAIL RUNNER. SHE'S PARTICIPATED IN (AND WON!) MANY INTERNATIONAL COMPETITIONS AND WAS AWARDED 'ADVENTURER OF THE YEAR 2017' BY NATIONAL GEOGRAPHIC.

JORDAN ROMERO

JORDAN ROMERO IS A MOUNTAIN CLIMBER FROM AMERICA. AT 13 YEARS OLD, HE SUMMITTED MOUNT EVEREST – THE HIGHEST MOUNTAIN IN THE WORLD.

YOUNG CHAMPS

JESSICA WATSON

JESSICA WATSON IS AN AUSTRALIAN SAILOR WHO RECEIVED AN ORDER OF AUSTRALIA MEDAL FOR COMPLETING A SOLO CIRCUMNAVIGATION OF THE SOUTHERN HEMISPHERE AGED JUST SIXTEEN.

BIGGEST STADIUMS IN THE WORLD

1

MAY DAY STADIUM
Where: Pyongyang, North Korea | Capacity: **150,000**
Team: North Korean National Team

2

MELBOURNE CRICKET GROUND
Where: Melbourne, Australia | Capacity: **100,024**
Team: National team and exhibition matches

CAMP NOU
Where: Barcelona, Spain | Capacity: **99,354**
Team: FC Barcelona

ESTADIO AZTECA
Where: Mexico City, Mexico | Capacity: **87,000**
Team: Mexican national team and Club América

3

4

5

6

AZADI STADIUM
Where: Tehran, Iran | Capacity: **78,116**
Team: Iranian national team, Esteghlal FC, & Persepolis FC

FNB STADIUM
Where: Johannesburg, South Africa | Capacity: **94,736**
Team: South African national team and Kaizer Chiefs

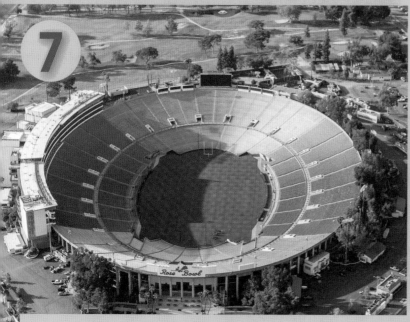

7

8

THE ROSE BOWL
Where: Pasadena, U.S.A. | Capacity: **92,542**
Team: UCLA Bruins

WEMBLEY STADIUM
Where: London, UK | Capacity: **90,000**
Team: English national team

GELORA BUNG KARNO STADIUM
Where: Jakarta, Indonesia | Capacity: **88,083**
Team: Indonesian national team

10

9

BUKIT JALIL NATIONAL STADIUM
Where: Kuala Lumpur, Malaysia | Capacity: **87,411**
Team: Malaysian national team

MAD Mascots

WORLD CUP WILLIE became one of the first official mascots when **FIFA** used the **Lion** as the symbol for their **1966 World Cup** tournament.

The five **MILWAUKEE BREWERS' SAUSAGE MASCOTS** take part in a **race** between the top and bottom of the sixth inning of every home baseball game.

KINGSLEY the **Scary Sunburst** mascot of **Partick Thistle** was designed by artist **David Shrigley.**

JAXSON the mascot of the Jacksonville Jaguars American football team has been known to bungee into the stadium before a game!

>>>

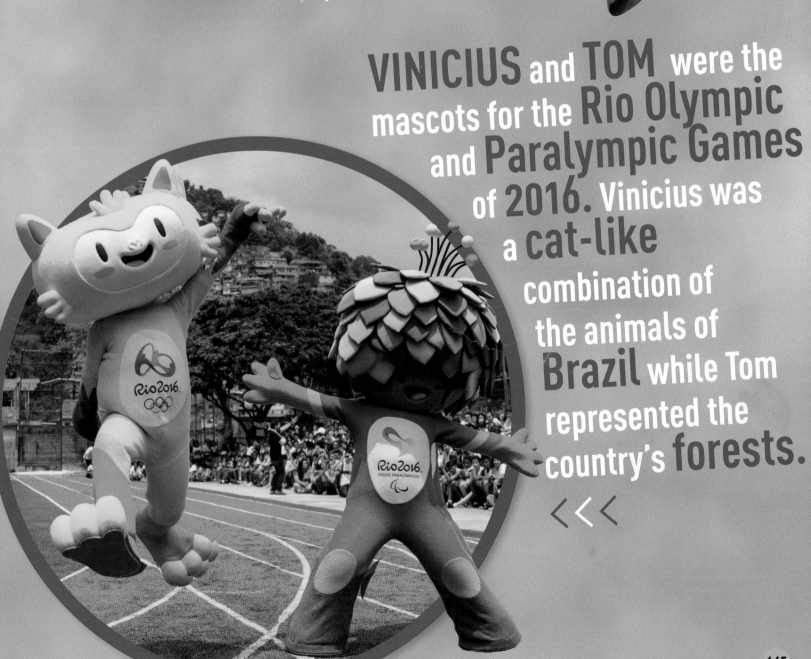

VINICIUS and TOM were the mascots for the Rio Olympic and Paralympic Games of 2016. Vinicius was a cat-like combination of the animals of Brazil while Tom represented the country's forests.

<<<

145

ZIP, ZIP, ZOOOOOM
WORLD'S FASTEST ZIP LINE

So you're standing on a perfectly good mountain and decide to throw yourself off it, head first. That may sound crazy, but that's what you need to do if you want to ride the

WORLD'S FASTEST ZIP LINE.

DO YOU DARE?

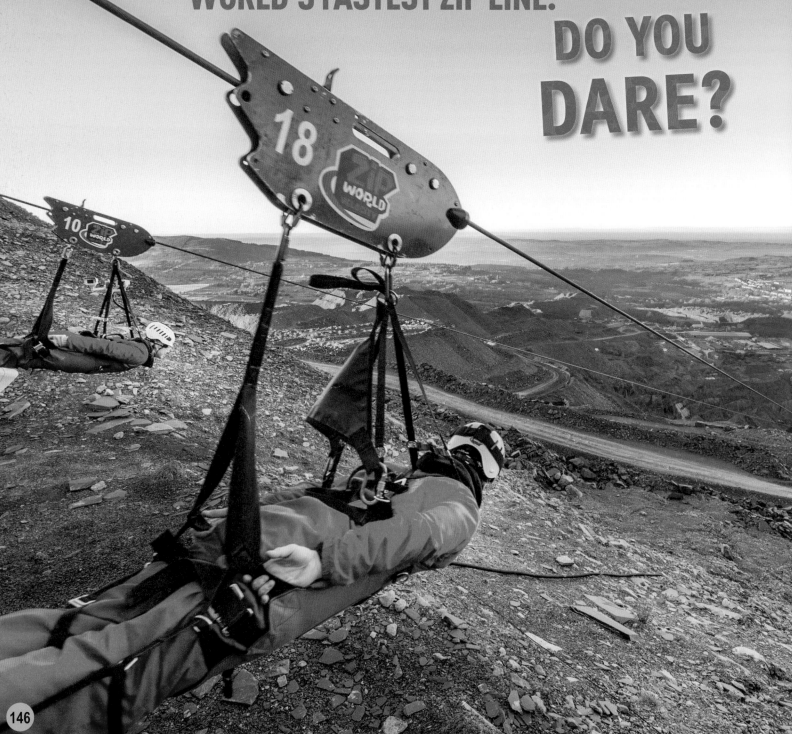

It's the fastest zip line in the world and the longest in Europe. In just a few seconds you'll be whizzing at 185 km/h (115 mph) with the ground a dizzying 150 m (490 ft) below you.

THINK YOUR MUM OR DAD ARE BRAVE ENOUGH?

In the **19th century** the **world's largest slate quarry** was dug into the mountain at **Penrhyn Quarry,** North Wales. It was **1.6 km** (1 mi) **long** and **370 m** (1,200 ft) **deep,** and was worked by nearly **3,000 quarrymen.** The hillside was almost hollowed out by the miners, which makes it the **perfect place to string up a zip line.**

PLAYING AWAY

SPORTS VENUES BUT NOT AS WE KNOW THEM

BASKET CASE

In 2011, the first-ever 'Carrier Classic' basketball game was held on the deck of the U.S.S. *Carl Vinson* aircraft carrier. The North Carolina Tar Heels beat the Michigan State Spartans 67–55, in front of 8,111 fans including President Obama.

PIN HIGH

Only one sport has been played on the moon – golf. In 1971, the commander of the Apollo 14 mission, Alan Shepard, sneaked a makeshift six-iron onto his spacecraft. When they reached the moon's surface he got out a couple of golf balls. His first shot ended up in a crater (even worse than a bunker!). But thanks to the moon's low gravity, he hit his second shot for 'miles and miles and miles'.

HITTING NEW HEIGHTS

Welcome to the world's highest tennis court. In 2005, Andre Agassi and Roger Federer played tennis on the helipad of the Burj al Arab hotel – 211 m (692 ft) above the shore of the Persian Gulf. Wouldn't fancy being the ball person for that game...

UNLIKELY ATHLETES

It's a dog's life not just human's! The annual **SURF CITY SURF DOG COMPETITION** in sunny California sees paddling pooches take to the waves!

FERRET LEGGING is about who can keep a ferret in their trousers the longest.

SWEDISH KANINHOP is a sport that encourages **rabbits** to do what rabbits do best – **hopping!** Bunnies have to complete a course with a **variety of jumps,** and if they're **not finished within two minutes,** they're **disqualified.**

Acro-yoga, combining **acrobatics** and **yoga,** is becoming very popular and has both **mental** and **physical** benefits.

Flick to page 157 to find out what happened when 150 acro-yoga fans got together.

Coolly CReaTiVE

UNUSUAL ORIGAMI

BIRDS OF A FEATHER

In 2016, a team of artists and technicians created 400 origami-like sculptures which open and close to mimic the flight patterns of birds.

CREATIVE CAMPAIGNING

Hundreds of origami birds were hung outside the Spanish Parliament building in Madrid to campaign for protection of Donana National Park, a UNESCO World Cultural and Natural Heritage site. The park, in which thousands of species of birds migrate through, is under threat, prompting creative campaigners to intervene. The campaign was supported by 130,000 people worldwide.

URBAN AMBUSH

Forgotten something?

Something started by seven people as a joke in 2001 has become a worldwide phenomenon – No Trousers on the Train Day. In 2016, hundreds of people over 60 cities took part – 300 people on the London Underground even participated.

Fan fever

Russian fans of the Korean rapper Psy celebrated his arrival in Moscow with a performance of his signature 'Gangnam Style' dance.

Namaste

In March 2016, 150 acro-yoga enthusiasts from across Israel gathered in Tel Aviv's Habima Square for what organisers dubbed the 'largest acro-yoga flash mob in the world'.

SHORT STORIES
Young authors making it big

GIANT FOLLOWING

Award-winning YouTuber **TYLER OAKLEY** has over seven million followers. His first book, *Binge,* has sold over 200,000 copies.

YOUNG MIND

On record for being the youngest author ever, **DOROTHY STRAIGHT** was published at six years old. The story was written when she was four as a present for her grandmother. It's called *How the World Began* and is said to have been written in just one evening!

ONLINE SENSATION

Scottish teenager **ESTELLE MASKAME** started putting her writing online when she was 13. She quickly gained thousands of followers, and in 2015 published her first book, *Did I Mention I Love You?*

VIDEO STAR

ZOE SUGG, also known as Zoella, became a published author when she was 23. Not only this, but her first book, *Girl Online,* was the fastest-selling book by a debut author ever, selling 78,109 copies in the first week!

TALKING PICTURES

The word **emoji** means 'picture' (e) + 'character' (moji) in **Japanese**.

Emoji was recognised as the UK's fastest-growing language in 2015.

In **China**, the **waving hand emoji** means 'bye, you're not my friend anymore'. A company in London has recently **employed an emoji translator**.

Earlier in 2017, **activists** in **New Zealand** used **inflatable poo emojis** to **protest** against how the government is **handling** the **environment**.

French people use **four times** as many **heart emojis** than those in other countries.

The **first emoji** was designed by **Shigetaka Kurita** in **1999**. At first there were only **200**; today there are **more than 1,000**.

In **2016**, a **Finnish town** considered naming two new roads 'Emoji Street' and 'Meme Street'.

A ;) was found in a *New York Times* transcript of an **1862 speech** given by **President Lincoln**. Historians are **unsure** if it was **intentional**, or **just a typo**. In the **UK**, the **winking emoji** is used **twice as much as** the world average.

DUCK ON TOUR

Dutch artist Florentijn Hofman's largest Rubber Duck is taller than a six-storey building, 20 metres (65 feet) wide, 23 metres (75 feet) long, and weighs 11 tonnes (24,000 lb). The duck in the photo is in Seoul, South Korea, but these rubber ducks have been everywhere from New Zealand to Canada.

SMART ART

GOT THE BUG?

Luke Jerram has made glass sculptures of viruses. Photographs of these are now used in a lot of medical journals.

STRANGE STONES

Are these pork cutlets? Actually, these hunks of meaty-looking art are stones, showcased at the 2017 'Strange Stone Exhibition' in Huaibei, China.

MINIMUM MONUMENT

Brazilian Néle Azevedo's 'Minimum Monument' are made up of tiny carved ice people. Passers by help assemble the monuments which eventually melt. The monument pictured signified the sacrifice of men and women in WWI.

MINI MOZART

She composed her **first piano sonata** at the age of **six**. At **seven**, she **wrote an opera**. At **nine**, a **concerto for violin**. But now musical prodigy **ALMA DEUTSCHER** has completed and performed in her **first full-length opera, *Cinderella*.** The opera had its premiere in Vienna, where it received a **standing ovation from the audience.**

As well as being a talented composer, she is also **skilled at the piano** and **violin**, and has a **YouTube channel** that has **millions of followers**, amongst them **Stephen Fry.** Currently she is working on finishing a piano concerto and is **writing a novel.**

WOLFGANG MOZART was also a bit of a **child prodigy.** He could **play multiple instruments** from a very young age, and by the **age of six** he was **playing to the public.** He went on to become one of the **most famous composers in the world.**

CREATIVE MASTERS

Facts you didn't know about plays, maps, and music...

Was that it?

Samuel Beckett wrote the shortest play. Called *Breath*, it lasts less than one minute!

Did you know tha Steve Reich composed a piece of music that is entirely made up of clapping?

Mapped out

In **2014** the **Ordnance Survey,** who make maps of the British isles, released a **complete map** of **Great Britain** in **Minecraft.** The map uses more than **83 billion blocks.** It is the **largest real-world place** created in the best-selling video game.

A **song** called **'Longplayer'** is the **longest-running piece of music ever. It began at midnight on 31st December 1999,** and it is **set to last 1000 years without repeating.** The song is being played using **singing bowls** in a **19th-century lighthouse** in **London.**

We'll never hear the end of this

Pigs have been hunting out **truffles** for humans since the Roman Empire.

Pigs are particularly suited to hunting for truffles. Head over to page 180 to find out why.

gRuB's uP!

INTERNATIONAL NOSH

School lunches from around the globe

BRAZIL
Feijoada, a dish of black beans cooked with beef and pork, served with rice.

CZECH REPUBLIC
Goulash soup with meat and potatoes, with a side of skubanky – potato dumplings with sugar and poppy seeds.

AUSTRALIA
Vegemite and butter sandwiches, with fruit and vegetables, and a chocolate bar.

INDIA
Steamed rice and lentil cakes, called idli, served with sambar – a lentil-based vegetable stew.

NIGERIA

Jollof rice – rice cooked with tomatoes and different spices – served with fried plantain.

SOUTH KOREA

Boiled rice, a noodle soup with mushrooms and seaweed, a salad, and kimchi – fermented spicy cabbage.

MARTHA PAYNE

Scottish schoolgirl Martha Payne started writing about her school lunches on her blog 'NeverSeconds' when she was in primary school. She began sharing school lunches sent in by children all over the world and her blog became very popular. It was even talked about in the news. Through the blog Martha raised more than £90,000 for Mary's Meals – a charity that gives school lunches to children in poor countries.

AHOY, THERE!

Find out what's on board the
WORLD'S LARGEST CRUISE SHIP

Modern cruise ships are the size of a small town. This ship is 362 metres (1,188 feet) long – that's the size of three and a half football pitches.

Every week, this ship has up to 6,780 guests set sail on a cruise. They all need three meals a day, plus snacks and treats (they're on holiday after all!), and it has to be loaded before they cast off.

On this cruise ship, there are 18 decks, 20 restaurants, 4 swimming pools, and 2,300 crew.

60,000 EGGS
1.1 TONNES OF FRESH SALMON
900 KG OF LOBSTER TAIL
450 LITRES OF CHOCOLATE ICE CREAM
21,000 ICE CREAM CONES
3.3 TONNES OF CHEESE
860 KG OF COFFEE
8 TONNES OF BEEF
9 TONNES OF CHICKEN
6.7 TONNES OF POTATOES
4 TONNES OF LETTUCE
12,000 LITRES OF MILK
10,700 HOT DOGS
16,900 CANS OF FIZZY DRINKS

ONE PINT (473mL)

Here is a typical weekly shopping list for the world's largest cruise ship

ALL HANDS ON DECK

So while you and your family are **playing mini-golf, splashing around** in one of the many on-board **pools,** or watching a **movie,** below decks, the **1,060-strong team** of **chefs** and **waiting staff** are **working very hard** indeed to get the **next mammoth meal** ready.

Fuelling the fittest

The **average man** needs **2,500 calories** to power his body through a day, and the **average woman** needs **2,000 calories**. But if you're a **superstar athlete** you **need more** – a lot more – if you're going to win races and beat records.

Usain Bolt

Sport: **track and field**

Average calorie count: **5,500 calories**

Many top athletes like to avoid fast food, but at the 2008 Beijing Olympics, sprinter Usain Bolt wolfed down chicken nuggets and fries for breakfast, lunch, and dinner, as well as an apple pie for a snack. He won two gold medals.

Serena & Venus Williams

Sport: tennis

Average calorie count: 3,500 calories each

Serena and Venus Williams follow a mostly vegan diet. They get their strength from beans, nuts, and lentils, as well as kale smoothies mixed with protein powder. And their favourite snack? Popcorn!

Michael Phelps

Sport: swimming

Average calorie count: up to 12,000 calories

Michael Phelps has won more Olympic medals than anyone else – including 23 golds – and has set 39 world records. To do this, he needs 12,000 calories a day – his breakfast alone consists of three fried-egg sandwiches, a five-egg omelette, a bowl of cereal, three slices of French toast, and three chocolate-chip pancakes. Imagine how much pasta he needs for his dinner...

Chris Froome

Sport: cycling

Average calorie count: 8,000 calories

Tour de France cyclists are in the saddle for hours each day over several weeks. To keep their energy levels up, they need about 8,000 calories a day. Cyclist Chris Froome starts his day with a huge bowl of porridge and berries, followed by an omelette and smoothie. He will then munch on jam sandwiches, rice cakes, gels, and sports drinks as he's cycling too.

175

INSECT EATING

Hungry? Then why not pop a pupa or two on your tongue?

The idea of eating insects **might seem freaky** to us, but humans have been guzzling insect eggs, larvae, pupae, and fully grown insects **since prehistoric times.**

FUN FACT

Fried tarantula spiders are a delicacy in Cambodia!

Feeling peckish?

In a way it's more unusual not to eat insects – **over 1,000 species** of **insects** are **eaten** by people in **80%** of the world's nations. Delicacies include crickets, cicadas, grasshoppers, caterpillars, ants, and beetle grubs. **Insects could be our food of the future.** They are **high in protein** and take **fewer resources to produce** than animal meat.

GRUB'S UP

YOU CAN NOW ORDER DRIED INSECTS ONLINE, AND IN 2015 THE UK'S FIRST INSECT RESTAURANT OPENED IN WALES. DINERS CAN ENJOY BUG BURGERS AND CRICKET KEBABS FOR MAIN; THEN FINISH WITH BAMBOO WORM FUDGE ICE CREAM FOR PUDDING!

SAVOUR THE FLAVOUR

These extraordinarily EXPENSIVE FOODS might set you back a pretty penny, but they're DEVOURED by people around the world. Satisfy your TASTE BUDS with these marvellous meals.

ELEPHANT POO COFFEE

£1,442 per kilogram

Brewed from number two! Elephants snack on coffee beans, which ferment in their stomachs for three days before they're passed and ready to be collected. It takes about 15 kilograms of coffee beans to make just 0.45 kilograms of coffee.

DENSUKE WATERMELON

up to £3,799

Densuke watermelons are very rare indeed – in Japan in 2008, only 100 were farmed and they sold for £3,799 each.

IRANIAN SAFFRON

£5,000 per 100g

This splendid spice, made from a flower called a crocus, has been treasured for thousands of years. It's been used as a medicine, in perfume, and for dying clothes. Cleopatra even took saffron-infused baths!

WHITE TRUFFLE

up to £10,000 per kilogram

Nicknamed the 'white diamond', this magnificent mushroom is one of the most expensive foods on Earth. They only grow underground, so most truffle hunters use trained dogs or pigs to find them.

SQUARE WATERMELON

£160 each

Some markets in Japan have crazy-shaped fruits, like this square watermelon. They come at a hefty price though!

TRUFFLE SNUFFLE
HUNTING FOR TRUFFLES

Truffles are fungi that grow in the forests of many countries including France, Spain, and Italy. They are very tasty but also very rare, which makes them expensive – that's where pigs come in. When truffles are in the right state for eating, they give off a particular smell that pigs are good at detecting.

Pigs are naturally good at using their snouts to root around for food. At the tip of their snout is a large round disk of cartilage, which is connected to a strong muscle. This makes the snout super-flexible and strong – ideal for rooting in the ground. Pigs can be trained to snuffle out truffles as deep as a metre underground. The only problem is that they also love scoffing the fabulous fungi, so when a pig finds a truffle, its owner has to quickly stop the creature from gobbling up the valuable fungus!

TRUFFLE TRIVIA

In 2014, the largest truffle ever was unearthed in central Italy. It weighed 1.9 kg (4.2 lb) and sold for nearly £39,154.

A PIZZA 20 TIMES LONGER THAN WEMBLEY?

Everyone loves pizza, right?

Not as much as these volunteers in California, U.S.A. The group of pizza bakers and pizza oven makers came together to create the **WORLD'S LONGEST PIZZA.** Measuring **2.13 km** (1.32 mi) in length, it would stretch the length of Wembley football pitch . . . **20 times over!**

5 BILLION PIZZAS

sold worldwide each year.

3 BILLION

of which are in the

U.S.A.

49%

of people in the U.K.

eat pizza at least once a week!

Squid is one of the most popular pizza toppings in Japan.

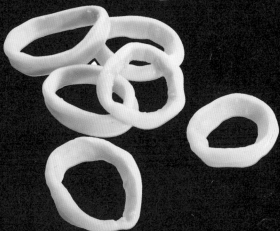

Hungry holidays

Feeling peckish but not sure WHAT TO SNACK ON? Grab your fork and whip out your calendar. There are FUN, FOODIE HOLIDAYS EVERY DAY OF THE YEAR! Check out some of the WILDEST and WACKIEST food holidays that celebrate tasty treats.

February 15th
GUMDROP DAY

April 26th
PRETZEL DAY

March 27th
PAELLA DAY

January 15th
STRAWBERRY
ICE CREAM DAY

May 28th

HAMBURGER DAY

June 4th

DOUGHNUT DAY

August 3rd

WATERMELON DAY

July 29th

FRENCH FRIES DAY

September 12th

CHOCOLATE MILKSHAKE DAY

October 1st

COFFEE DAY

November 3rd

SANDWICH DAY

December 1st

RED APPLE DAY

index

191

SUBSCRIBE TODAY!

Visit our new website natgeokids.com or call 01795 412847

Love National Geographic Kids? Have you enjoyed our free sample iPad edition from the App Store? Well, sign up to the magazine, iPad edition or BOTH today and save money!

PRINT ONLY

£30

A subscription to *National Geographic Kids* magazine is the perfect gift for boys and girls aged six and over. Packed with features about nature, science, geography, history and popular culture, **Nat Geo Kids** gets children excited about the world. It helps with their homework, too!

Regular price £50
QUOTE CODE **NGKWBT**

FULL SUBSCRIPTION

PREMIUM

£40

This premium package will keep kids entertained for hours while teaching them about the amazing world we live in. Subscribe to both *National Geographic Kids* magazine and the interactive **Nat Geo Kids iPad app** and you'll save £40!

Regular price £80
QUOTE CODE **NGKWBTB**

DIGITAL ONLY

£20

The **National Geographic Kids iPad app** is jam-packed with videos, games, sounds and extra interactive content that really bring *National Geographic Kids* magazine to life! Engaging and exciting, **Nat Geo Kids' iPad edition** makes learning more fun than ever!

Regular price £30
QUOTE CODE **NGKWBTD**

NATIONAL GEOGRAPHIC KiDS